THE SQUADRON THAT DIED TWICE

GORDON THORBURN

THE SQUADRON THAT DIED TWICE

THE STORY OF NO. 82
SQUADRON RAF, WHICH IN 1940
LOST 23 OUT OF 24 AIRCRAFT
IN TWO BOMBING RAIDS

metro

First published by Metro Publishing,
an imprint of
John Blake Publishing Limited
3 Bramber Court, 2 Bramber Road
London W14 9PB

www.johnblakepublishing.co.uk

www.facebook.com/johnblakebooks ⬛f
twitter.com/jblakebooks ⬛t

First published in hardback in 2015

ISBN: 978-1-78418-419-3

British Library Cataloguing-in-Publication Data:

A catalogue record for this book is available from the British Library.

Design by www.envydesign.co.uk

Printed in Great Britain by CPI Group (UK) Ltd

1 3 5 7 9 10 8 6 4 2

Papers used by John Blake Publishing are natural, recyclable products made
from wood grown in sustainable forests. The manufacturing processes conform to
the environmental regulations of the country of origin.

Every attempt has been made to contact the relevant copyright-holders,
but some were unobtainable. We would be grateful if the appropriate
people could contact us.

CONTENTS

ACKNOWLEDGEMENTS

Grateful thanks are due to Julian Horn, historian of RAF Watton and 82 Squadron, who provided photographs, the letter from Freddie Thripp and much besides; Peter Cornwell for research into the events of 17 May; John Lart for new information on his uncle; and Søren Flensted, Jørn Junker and Carsten Petersen for photographs.

Above all, many thanks to Ole Bang Rønnest, for photographs and without whose meticulous research (he is a retired Danish police CSI officer) on the Ålborg raid an accurate story would have been impossible. With Ole's permission, his own account of the raid, recorded some years ago when he was able to contact some of the survivors, has been heavily mined for this book.

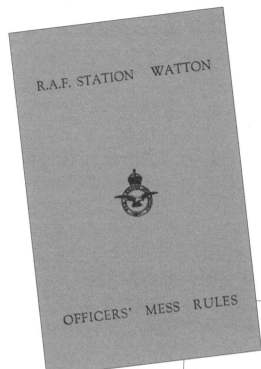

'It is customary not to mention Ladies' names at dinner.' Cover and pages from the RAF Station, Watton Officers' Mess Rules.

Mess Rules
SECTION I.

Membership.

1. Every Commissioned Officer of the R.A.F., W.A.A.F., Royal Navy or Army, posted to or attached to the Station, whether resident or non resident, shall be a member of the Officers' Mess.

2. Every unmarried Officer, save in exceptional circumstances approved by the Station Commander, shall be a resident member of the Mess.

Temporary Membership.

3. All officers serving in the R.A.F., other than those belonging to the Station, shall become temporary members when visiting the Mess.

Honorary Membership.

4. Civilian Officials of Officer grade attached to the Station, may be invited, after approval by a General Mess Meeting and the Station Commander, to become Honorary Members.

5. Subject to these rules, honorary members will enjoy the full privilege of the Mess, excepting they will not be eligible to attend or vote at Mess Meetings. Honorary members may invite guests to the Mess, or to meals in the Mess.

THREE

PREFACE

These rules are issued in accordance with and in amplification of Chapter 22, Section 1, of King's Regulations and Air Council Instructions, and A.P. 128 "Standard Rules for Royal Air Force Officers' Messes."

.... A CDR.

Commandant.

Mess Staff.

17. The duties of Mess Staff are laid down by the P.M.C. and Mess Committee. Members of the Mess are not to order Mess Staff to carry out other duties nor to send them out of the Mess with messages. There may be occasions when a member will find it necessary to check a member of the staff for not carrying out his or her duties properly, or for misbehaviour. Should this be necessary, the member of the Mess concerned should also report the matter to the Mess Secretary in writing. Matters connected with the general efficiency and behaviour of Mess Staff are not to be raised directly between members and the staff, but are to be referred to the Mess Secretary in writing. The Mess Secretary and the Committee will then be responsible for dealing with the matters raised and taking action with the Mess Staff concerned.

Batmen and Batwomen.

18. Officers' batmen or batwomen are available, if required, for Mess duties. An Officer keeping his servant away from Mess duties, after he has been duly warned, will be required to explain his action to the Mess Committee.

Dress.

19. The wearing of war service dress in the Mess is not permitted after 19.00 hours.

20. Civilian clothes may be worn after duty hours, except on Dining in Nights or during official Mess functions, when the uniform as ordered is to be worn.

21. An officer is responsible to the President for the dress of any friends he may bring into the Mess.

22. No officer is permitted in public rooms of the Mess dressed in sports kit—i.e. shorts, jerseys, etc.

Dining In Nights.

23 (1) An official Dining in Night will be held once a month. This dinner is a parade and Officers will be detailed to the capacity of the dining room.

(2) All members attending will be in the ante room one half hour before the time of dinner. On arrival he will pay his respects in the normal way to the Senior Officer present.

(3) No smoking will be permitted in the ante room before dinner. "Long" drinks will not be served.

(4) Officers will follow the President in to dinner in the order of their seniority. Any seat may be occupied, except those allocated to the President and Vice President and Station Commander.

(5) Members may not leave the table without the permission of the President. General permission "granted" is indicated by the President rising and then resuming his seat again.

(6) No smoking is to take place at dinner until the wine has been passed and the President's permission obtained.

(7) It is customary not to mention Ladies' names at dinner.

(8) Dress will be No. 1 blue service dress, white shirts and collars with bow tie, or mess undress kit.

(9) On dining in nights and other occasions, at the discretion of the President, His Majesty's health is to be drunk, as ordered in K.R. and A.C.I. On these occasions the President calls for silence, and then, rising, says, "Mr. Vice, The King!" The vice president then rises, and when he is standing, replies, "Gentleman, The King." When all have risen, the toast is drunk. If a band is in attendance, the National Anthem is to be played immediately after the vice president has called the toast and when all are standing. The toast is not to be drunk, nor are glasses to be lifted, until the anthem has been played. Other toasts are to be given after "The King." The dining in nights, when the band is present and when the toasts are finished, the bandmaster may be invited by the president of the week to join him at table for a glass of wine.

SECTION IV.

Hours of Closing.

24. The Mess is to be closed by 00.01 hours, unless permission has previously been given by the Station Commander.

SECTION V.

Mess Management.

25. A Mess Committee will be appointed to manage the affairs of the Mess, and will consist of a President and at least three members. The President of the Mess Committee will be appointed by the Station Commander ; the members of the Committee may be elected at a General Mess Meeting, at the discretion of the Station Commander.

26. The Mess Committee are responsible for the proper ordering and efficiency of all departments of the Mess, in accordance with the individual duties laid down in K.R. and A.C.I., Chapter XX, and for seeing that stocks of wines, tobaccos, groceries and cleaning materials are not maintained above normal requirements. They will maintain and organise the Mess for the general benefit and comforts of members, and carry into effect decisions reached at General Mess Meetings.

27. The Mess Secretary will settle all monthly and other accounts due to tradespeople and others by the 10th of the following month.

28. The P.M.C. is empowered to authorise all expenditure for the routine running of the Mess, but he will not order any plate or furniture, or authorise any extraordinary expenditure against the Mess exceeding £20

CHAPTER ONE

THE FLYING MACHINE

The eighty-second squadron of the Royal Flying Corps was formed at Doncaster on 7 January 1917 and moved to France and the Great War in November, based in the Aisne and Oise areas of the Western Front. Matters such as squadron mottoes and badges were not uppermost in wartime minds and, for some reason now forgotten, No. 82's badge was a picture of a steaming kettle with the sun in the background. Squadron equipment was the Armstrong Whitworth FK8, so named because it was one of a series designed by Dutch engineer Frederick Koolhoven. Like all Royal Flying Corps machines not specifically designed as fighters, it was a general-purpose, workhorse type of biplane expected to defend itself if necessary. Called by its airmen Big Ack, it was not as well known nor as widely used as the Royal Aircraft Factory RE8 (called Harry Tate) but was more popular with pilots.

Compared with the fighters on both sides, such machines were big and slow – consider the FK8's wingspan of 43 feet and top speed of 95mph against the SE5A's 26 feet and 140mph or, more to the point, the Fokker DVII at 29 feet and 125mph – but the FK8, RE8 and the BE2 that went before were not meant for aerial combat. They were steady, reliable platforms for reconnaissance, bombing (such as it was then), spotting for the artillery and 'contact patrols' – very low flying following the progress of infantry advances on 'battle days'. The FK8's speed was rather less than 95mph when fully loaded with its 260lb of bombs. Its main defence was a Lewis gun fired by the observer; its additional fixed, forward-facing Vickers machine gun could be fired by the pilot but rarely was except in strafing ground targets.

In the last months of the war, new uses were found for the FK8, such as dropping supplies to the advancing Allied troops, but the Armistice signalled the end of the aircraft's useful life and the temporary end of 82 Squadron.

Before 1920 was out, the British air force, now the RAF, had been reduced to one fighter squadron and four army co-operation squadrons at home; five Imperial policing squadrons in Egypt, four more in each of India and Iraq and one in the Far East. In round numbers, 23,000 officers, 21,000 cadets and 227,000 other ranks had been demobilised and the Women's Royal Air Force disbanded.

The men-only RAF thus consisted of 3,280 officers and 25,000 other ranks, most of it overseas. More than 160 squadrons had been dissolved and dismissed, and the next few years were characterised by attacks on the RAF itself:

by the two other armed services and by those politicians and commentators who thought it too expensive for Britain to afford. Its success in policing the Empire in a most economical fashion and, curiously, government concerns about the intentions of the old enemy, France, which had retained a much bigger air force, ensured the survival of the RAF with a capacity for both defence – fighters – and offence, bombers.

A question for the air force and the government was – what sort of bombers? Did they want big machines that could carry heavy loads to lay waste large areas, or smaller ones that could dart in and out of specific targets, delivering swift tactical blows?

Here is a French expert, Georges Prade, writing in 1916. He classifies four uses for, and therefore types of, military aircraft: reconnaissance scouts, artillery observation machines, battleplanes (fighters or chasers), and bomb-droppers:

> The bomb-dropper is the Dreadnought of the air. It must include among its qualities a certain minimum of speed, climbing power, and manoeuvring capacity to enable it to escape from the fire of anti-air guns. As for chasers, bomb-droppers must not be expected to defend themselves against these. They must be escorted by squadrons which have nothing else to do. Bombarding fleets [should] always include several squadrons, operating on well-determined itineraries, known in advance, at fixed hours. Thus, convoying them is easy. It has been found possible to group in this way 50 machines, which, flying in a triangle

like wild duck, have gone as far as the large cities of South Germany [from France]. These machines must therefore have powerful motors – 200 h.p. – a large range of action, and large fuselage, permitting the well-aimed dropping of bombs by special apparatus. They should also carry a machine gun.

This is the most difficult machine to construct, and the task of he who pilots it is both ungrateful and perilous – long raids over enemy territory.

Monsieur Prade was of the opinion that bomber meant heavy bomber, escorted by fighters, and the RAF agreed to an extent. All the way through the 1920s and most of the 1930s, large, slow biplanes were strategic equipment, for example the Vickers Virginia, a machine closely resembling and hardly outperforming the Vickers Vimy of 1917.

By 1936, the threat from Germany was becoming rather more obvious, but Britain had no aircraft that would have been able to fly to Germany from home ground, deliver a usefully damaging amount of bombs, and get back again. The RAF went into a period of expansion and the new RAF Commands were formed – Fighter, Bomber, Coastal and Training – with the Commands split into Groups according to primary task and aircraft type. No. 3 Group of Bomber Command would have the heavy bombers, such as they might be, while 1 and 2 Groups would fly the light bombers for supporting ground forces.

It was obvious to bomber strategists that their job would be a hard one. All thought was of precision targets; that meant going in daylight because such targets could not be found at night. If they were to go in daylight, the only way they could reach their targets would be if they could defend themselves against fighter attack and somehow avoid the shooting from the ground.

Flying in close formation, with cloud cover, could be the answer if clouds could be predicted accurately, or at all, and if it were possible to keep formation in the clouds when bomber crews couldn't see each other. Keeping formation while attacking, and while under attack, would be even more difficult, which made things doubly questionable when the tight formation was the given means of defence.

Flying too quickly for the ground gunners would also be good, if only there were an aircraft that could go that fast. Having long-range fighter escorts would also be very welcome, if only such were available.

German targets did not become practicable until the faster, monoplane light bombers began coming into service in 1937: the Vickers Wellesley (180mph, 2,000lb bombs), the Fairey Battle (260mph, 1,000lb bombs) and the Bristol Blenheim (269mph, 1,000lb bombs Mark I, 266mph, 1,000lb bombs plus 320lb bombs carried externally Mark IV,).

Bigger aircraft were wanted too, and they came in around the same time: the Armstrong Whitworth Whitley (220mph, 7,000lb bombs), the Handley Page Hampden (250mph, 4,000lb bombs) and, at last, the Vickers Wellington (240mph, 4,500lb bombs).

H P Folland, designer of the SE5A and Gloster Gladiator biplane fighters, wrote in June 1939: 'Present heavily loaded bombers of the multi-engined type are, and will be, at least 80mph slower than interceptor fighters, and I consider it very doubtful whether a sufficient number of machines would reach their target, except under special conditions such as in poor weather and at night.' So, long before the introduction of four-engined heavy bombers, he favoured the hit-and-run type of bomber, and he designed one (see diagram). Events were to prove him wrong.

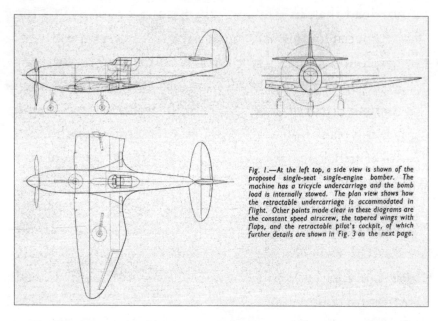

Fig. 1.—At the left top, a side view is shown of the proposed single-seat single-engine bomber. The machine has a tricycle undercarriage and the bomb load is internally stowed. The plan view shows how the retractable undercarriage is accommodated in flight. Other points made clear in these diagrams are the constant speed airscrew, the tapered wings with flaps, and the retractable pilot's cockpit, of which further details are shown in Fig. 3 on the next page.

Built for speed, Folland's single-seater hit-and-run bomber looks more like a Spitfire than a Lancaster, and it was large-scale strategic bombing that would be the way forward. Designs along Folland lines, such as the Fairey Battle and the Bristol Blenheim, which were neither fighter nor heavyweight bomber, would prove just how disastrously wrong was the Folland school of thought, at enormous cost to aircrew.

No. 82 Squadron was reformed as a light bomber unit in 2 Group, equipped with the Hawker Hind, at Andover on 14 June 1937. The Hind was an improved version of a 1920s design, the Hawker Hart, although the improvements did not result in better performance. It was still a small biplane, less than 40 feet wingspan, able to fly at 185mph and carrying only 500lb of bombs. It was decidedly an interim measure while those better aircraft mentioned above were in development.

The squadron was not alone in being ill-equipped. All the 2 Group bombers were biplanes, mostly without wireless sets, armed with a couple of machine guns and carrying a war load that, in size and composition, was suitable only for Imperial duties. As an anonymous contributor wrote in a contemporary edition of *Encyclopaedia Britannica*, 'Aircraft have proved of the utmost value for the control of semicivilised or uncivilised countries and for carrying out those classes of wars which may be grouped under the term of tribal operations.' The classes of war for which 82 Squadron was formed could not have been so grouped.

The strength of the 'new' squadron was thirteen each of officers, senior NCOs and corporals, and fifty-three of lower ranks. The first commanding officer was Squadron Leader Norman Charles 'Shorty' Pleasance who, as Group Captain and station commander of RAF Waddington, would be killed in a 9 Squadron Lancaster on an operation to Frankfurt on 22 March 1944, flying as sightseeing passenger with Flying Officer Albert Manning. Although liable to get in a lather when under pressure, Shorty Pleasance was generally well regarded, a nice old boy, approachable. He'd done his years of Empire protection on the North West Frontier and, later, would run a large part of the pilot training programme in Canada. At 9 Squadron, with no need to go on ops at all, he was killed on his third trip trying to keep in touch with what his boys were facing routinely.

Andover was 82 Squadron's base for only three weeks, before moving to Cranfield, Bedfordshire, where they formed a station with 108 and 62 Squadrons. All three flew the old biplanes, had accidents including one fatality, and waited for the new aircraft to turn up.

That better machine arrived at 82 Squadron in 1938, the Bristol Blenheim, a quite remarkable advance on what had gone before. Not only was it a hundred miles an hour faster than the Hind; it was faster than the fighters then in service with the RAF, which were biplanes such as the Gloster Gladiator. If anyone noticed that the Messerschmitt Bf 109 was already in service with the Luftwaffe, an aircraft that had set a new speed record of almost 380mph, the implications for the Blenheim were not fully understood.

Rather, the Blenheim was seen as a very exciting aircraft, superfast, super-modern, the best bomber in an unsettled continent – which it was, at the time. Its origins, however, lay not in any Air Ministry specification but in the foresight of the Bristol Aeroplane Company, leading it to design a small, high-speed passenger plane in 1933, and in the desire of a wealthy businessman for something revolutionary, a fast, luxurious, executive aircraft.

The Bristol Type 135 would be a low-wing monoplane, carrying two crew and eight passengers. It would have all-metal construction and two 500hp nine-cylinder Bristol Aquila engines. The non-flying full-scale model was put on show at the 1935 International Air Show in Paris.

Meanwhile, Lord Rothermere, the flamboyant owner of the *Daily Mail*, expressed his wish for an aeroplane that would carry him and five colleagues quickly to wherever he wanted to go. His money and the Type 135 were soon united in the redesignated Bristol Type 142, with more powerful engines and a sleeker shape to achieve the range that his lordship required. Rothermere ended up with a bill for £18,500, roughly £5 million in today's money.

Rothermere's machine, named *Britain First*, flew at Filton on 12 April 1935. It was a spectacular success, 30mph faster than the Gloster Gauntlet, the recently introduced open-cockpit biplane fighter that was then the RAF's speediest aircraft. The Air Ministry asked if they could have *Britain First* for a while, to see if it might be converted to a bomber, and Lord Rothermere agreed. Harold Harmsworth, first Viscount Rothermere, was a noted Nazi sympathiser, later writing to Hitler to congratulate him on annexing Czechoslovakia, but he did recognise the longer-term military threat to Great Britain. He also believed that modern aerial bombardment would defeat and ruin a country in short order, a possibility for which Britain was very ill prepared. So, despite his admiration for the new Germany, he presented *Britain First* to the nation.

RAF trials at Martlesham Heath, Suffok, were so promising that the Air Ministry issued Specification B28/35 for a military version. Bristol's answer to the spec was accepted and an order placed for 150 aircraft in September 1935. The main changes to Lord Rothermere's executive carriage were a bomb-aimer's station, a bomb bay and a dorsal gun turret, more powerful engines (Bristol Mercury VIII) and movement of the wings to mid-fuselage. The prototype flew on 25 June 1936, official trials began that October and the first deliveries to squadrons of the Blenheim, as it now was, started in March 1937.

Pilot and observer/navigator/bomb-aimer sat at the front while the wireless operator/air gunner (WOp/AG) was jammed into the turret. The bomb bay was in the wing centre-section; defensive weaponry was a fixed .303 inch Browning machine-gun in the port wing and a single Vickers .303 machine-gun in the turret. Range with war load was said to be 1,125 miles and/or five and a half hours.

Speed had been at the heart of the design. The results in terms of crew accommodation might have been halfway reasonable for a civil version, meant only to flip his lordship and guests from meeting to meeting, but the slim fuselage and the pointed nose gave very little room for a crew to go to war. The pilot's view was quite restricted, especially of the ground while landing and of his instruments while flying. Some controls were behind his back.

The WOp/AG had responsibility for his gun, his transmitter/receiver – a primitive machine by later standards requiring constant attention and a certain amount of inspiration to keep it working – and for much else of the electrics, including lights and the intercom. The intercom was very important indeed, the sound of the engines being loud enough to deafen all inside the aircraft. The WOp/AG was physically isolated too; crawling space between the nose and the turret was cramped by the main spar. In battle, the observer/navigator, say, trying to reach a wounded gunner would have had to take his parachute off to get through, and wouldn't have had room to do anything very helpful should he have managed it.

For the single machine gun, the WOp/AG had 1,600 rounds of ammunition, ordinary .303 rifle bullets, carried in pans of 100 rounds. The theoretical firing rate of 1,200 rounds a minute may have been faster than its direct German equivalent but it was nothing compared to the thousands a minute of a Messerschmitt's combined cannon and guns. Firing and pan-changing in combat would prove to be an intensive activity for the poor WOp/AG.

The observer – and navigator/bomb-aimer – had a very cramped office with no room for a proper chart table. As was the case throughout the RAF and the Luftwaffe, he had no navigation aids of any kind, beyond the traditional ones of eyes, map, compass and timepiece, and stars on a clear night if he carried his own sextant. His bombsight showed only minor technical advance on the Wimperis Course Setting Bomb Sight used in the old biplane bombers that flew 150mph slower than he did and with smaller bombs.

Bomb bays were of the old type too, with doors held shut by elastic cords. When the bombs were released, they fell on the doors, forced them open and then, after a small but important amount of time that could only be estimated, dropped towards the target. If there was a mathematical formula for calculating air speed with wind speed with weight of bombs versus strength of bungee cords at X thousand feet, bomb-aimers didn't know it and so pinpoint accuracy could not be achieved at any kind of safe height, although it was often expected.

This basic problem was not really recognised at the time, because all bombing practice was on precision targets, unopposed of course, often at low level. There was no possibility of simulating attack from Wehrmacht anti-aircraft guns and Messerschmitt fighters while the Blenheims flew straight and level at a convenient height in their attempts to hit a certain oil refinery.

The pilot was the captain, regardless of rank. It was possible that a sergeant pilot would have an officer observer, if unlikely, but the WOp/AG was almost certainly aircraftman rank, AC2 (Aircraftman Second Class), AC1 (Aircraftman First Class) or LAC (Leading Aircraftman). For the pilot, changing from the machines he knew like the Hind and the Avro Anson to the Blenheim was something similar to passing your driving test in an Austin Seven then being given a Bentley Speed Six for your birthday.

The Anson was another development from a civil aircraft, an airliner that became an unsuitable bomber that turned into a trainer and reconnaissance machine. The Mark I was the first RAF plane with a retractable undercarriage, although pilots often forwent this facility as it required well over 100 turns on a hand-crank to bring up the wheels. When it came to the Blenheim, with hydraulic undercart retraction, pilots sometimes forgot they had no wheels on landing approaches and quite a few pancake crashes ensued, while the major differences in performance between Anson and Blenheim, especially in landing approach, also contributed to the wreckage. Both of these machines were entirely different again from the Hind.

The novelty was also a challenge for the ground crew. In this revolutionary aircraft, nothing was what they were used to except for the training which, for aircrew and ground crew alike, in the RAF style of the time, was based on the assumption that the chaps would soon work it out.

The first Blenheim to be delivered to an operational squadron crashed on landing and was a write-off, when the pilot was over-enthusiastic on the brakes and turned turtle, which could only contribute to the already burgeoning reputation the Blenheim had for not keeping itself in good shape. Some of these first machines were 'development' aircraft, expected to be flown for 500 hours as soon as possible and then returned to the factory for checks and tests. Aircraftman First Class Richard Passmore, WOp/AG, remembered one such:

> I did a fair amount of flying in K7059 and watched thoughtfully the steady deterioration of the visible surfaces, heard the creaks and groans accumulating, and felt more of that dicing-with-death feeling than normally. By the time she was ready to return to Bristol, the port wheel was lashed on with wire rope, everything rattled, and her condition was so unreassuring that the squadron's pilots drew lots for the honour of flying her on her last trip. The loser won, so to speak.

Factories at A V Roe and Rootes were brought in to help Bristol, and between them they built just short of 1,400 of the

Blenheim in its first version, equipping twenty-six squadrons at home and in Empire outposts.

The RAF now had some aircraft capable of attacking targets in Germany and would soon have more types capable in different ways. There were nowhere near enough for an all-out war, nor were there men to fly them should there ever be enough, nor yet a cohesive system for fully training such men. There were still no navigation aids beyond the old methods, so finding specific aiming points in bad weather or at night remained a matter of luck and inspiration. There was no stratagem for aircraft combining together to hit a marked target, and no devices for target marking, had there been such a stratagem. There were no RAF fighters that could do Germany and back but the idea that bombers could defend themselves successfully against enemy fighters had not been tried, much less proved. Worse, there had been no serious thinking about how these matters might be resolved.

Although a full-scale offensive of strategic bombing against Germany was to become the official policy, the RAF was a long, long way from being able to carry it out.

Air Chief Marshal Sir Edgar Ludlow-Hewitt, Commander-in-Chief of the bomber force from 1937, had had a brilliant career in the Great War, starting as a pilot of high repute and ending as a thirty-one-year-old brigadier, Royal Flying Corps. That he had a superb brain and exceptional talent for administration and analysis was never in doubt, though his abilities as a front-line commander were less apparent to some of his senior colleagues.

His own serious thinking, on the gap between policy and

ANOTHER ONE FOR DR. GOEBBELS' LIBRARY OF WAR PICTURES: *One of Britain's fleet of mighty war 'planes. This monster of the skies flies aloft at nearly 52 m.p.h. and is declared capable of crossing the Channel. Trained aeronauts are in charge of the machines. The principle of the engine is that of internal combustion. Britain now boasts proudly that she has not one steam-driven air-o'-plane left in the Royal Air Force. Her fleet of the up-to-date machines pictured here is upwards of 40. Each pilot is a Master of Arts and has reached the qualified age of 65.*

Doubt about the RAF's capability in a bombing war obviously extended beyond the corridors of power.

capability, came to a horribly obvious conclusion. His pleas for more resources did not resonate loudly enough with the Air Ministry, preoccupied as most officials and politicians were with the requirements of Fighter Command and, in any case, there was that general belief, summed up years before by Stanley Baldwin, that the bombers would always get through.

There was also opposition, or inertia, among those who objected to the whole business of bombing a country into submission. The RAF's plan for destroying industrial targets in the Ruhr was initially met with a ministerial objection that factories were private property.

Ludlow-Hewitt saw that if he were asked to mount that offensive, Bomber Command would be totally destroyed. With war approaching, he calculated that his current force would be annihilated within eight weeks. That force consisted of fifty-three squadrons of five types of aircraft – Wellington, Whitley, Hampden, Battle and Blenheim.

Aircrew comfort was never much of a priority in warplane design unless it impinged directly on effectiveness in action, and the Blenheim did leave much to be desired in that respect. A new nose was called for, so the pilot could see and do everything with minimum inconvenience, and the observer/bomb-aimer could do his job a lot better with more space and a chart table. The WOp/AG would appreciate a little more room and turret controls that were simpler and more convenient. Armament remained the same for the moment, although efforts to improve the machine defensively would later include twin guns in the turret and a fixed, rearwards firing gun under the nose.

More powerful Bristol XV engines and bigger fuel tanks gave the new Blenheim, the Mark IV, longer range (1,460 miles unloaded), making it more suitable for reconnaissance although it was still seen as a bomber, a role for which it was not so suitable. It was no faster than the Mark I (slightly slower in fact) but it seemed to many aircrew and senior officers the very model of the modern light bomber, especially in view of biplanes gone before.

These are official Air Ministry figures, showing how the air speed of bombers progressed in the ten years up to 1939, given in mph:

Type	1929	1934	1939
Light	Fox 160	Hart 184	Battle 257
Medium	Sidestrand 144	Overstrand 152	Blenheim 295
Heavy	Virginia 104	Heyford 142	Hampden 265
		Hendon 156	Wellington 265

The definition of a heavy bomber was really little more than the heartiest twin-engined beast around at that moment, and obviously does not compare with the later four-engined heavies. None of the 1934 bombers could have reached a target in Germany with a worthwhile bombload and got home again. Why the Blenheim was classified as medium is not clear, as the standard bombload was the same – 1,000lb – as before and the same as the Battle, and where they got 295mph from isn't clear either.

In December 1938, HM King George VI had approved the new 82 Squadron motto – *Super omnia ubique* (Over everything everywhere) – and the new badge, a weathercock in front of a sun in splendour, a nod to the original World War One design. This squadron was ready to operate in any direction, or it would be in August 1939, a month before war broke out, when the new Mark IV arrived and the move to Watton was made. Meanwhile, there were exercises in the Mark I, low-

and high-level bombing practice, cross-country flights, flying displays and, for 82 Squadron, ferrying Blenheims to RAF stations in Egypt. Squadrons from 2 and 3 Groups flew over France on missions to show solidarity and the flag; No. 82 did a round trip over Beachy Head to Paris, Orleans, Chartres and back, not realising just how well the crews would get to know such unfamiliar territory in the not too distant future.

As war drew closer, other jobs were found for the 1,400 or so Mark I Blenheims, some in training and some being converted to nightfighters, and the other home-based squadrons also re-equipped with the Mark IV. At least, that was the theory.

The actuality, two days before war was declared, was rather different. The RAF had been moving up through various official stages of readiness: Readiness D, 26 August, meant no flying except for necessary testing, aircraft dispersed around the outlying parts of airfields, all personnel recalled from leave, all aircraft to be serviceable. When mobilisation was ordered on the afternoon of 1 September, three of the 2 Group squadrons still had the Blenheim Mark I. Seven squadrons, including No. 82, had the Blenheim IV, but two of them (Nos 90 and 101) didn't have the new engines yet. Most of the rest had the larger petrol tanks fitted but half didn't have the new fuel systems completely installed.

Other technical hitches and incomplete facilities meant that 2 Group could offer only 82, 107, 110 and 139 Squadrons as ready for the fray. No. 82 had fourteen aircraft serviceable, and fifteen crews. In a general 'scattering' in expectation of German bombing raids, half of 82's strength was despatched to the satellite aerodrome at Horsham St Faith (now Norwich International Airport).

By this time, exercises with Spitfires and Hurricanes had shown that the Blenheim, faster than anything else in the RAF when it was designed, was now nowhere near fast enough. Still, there was nothing anybody could do about that.

No country has yet had extensive experience in modern aerial warfare, and although certain experience has been gained in the Spanish Civil War and in China, these can only be compared to an Air Force Pageant in relation to what aerial warfare between two powerful nations would be. (H P Folland, June 1939.)

To-day the aeroplanes supplied in quantity to the Royal Air Force are technically as good as, or better than, those in other air forces. (F Handley Page, President of the Society of British Aircraft Constructors, July 1939.)

Following recent successful experiments, a number of Italian reconnaissance machines will be equipped with television transmission sets enabling them to send off instantaneous pictorial reports of work done. The only problem still awaiting solution concerns the dimensions of the apparatus, which is very heavy. (*L'Aquilone* magazine, 13 August 1939.)

The invisible wall, the Air Defence Zone West, is unsurpassable. Raiding machines will either be brought down entering German territory, or leaving it. (German periodical *Der Adler*, 22 August 1939.)

CHAPTER TWO

A TIME AND A PLACE

During World War Two, a great many villages and small towns in East Anglia would find themselves transformed by the rapid addition to the local geography of a fighting aerodrome, but in Watton, Norfolk, the transformation came earlier, in peacetime, and not so suddenly.

The last time Watton had had such a buzz about the place was around the Elizabethan era, when wool was the business and Norwich was England's second city. This area of Norfolk, called Wayland, and the greater region, called Breckland, was always a candidate for outsider-mocking as the middle of nowhere. Unless you happened to be travelling between East Dereham and Thetford, you probably would never come across Watton, although you might know the story of the *Babes in the Wood*, supposedly originating in the ancient darknesses of Wayland forest.

This quiet old town made its living largely from arable

farming and life was geared to the annual cycle of the seasons. The people of Watton didn't bother much about the world beyond the horizon, but that world came to them in September 1936 when work began on a new aerodrome, just south of the Norwich road, east of the town centre, between the Watton outskirts and the village of Griston.

Work at 'the camp' paid rather better than agricultural labourers had been used to, and local farmers had to rethink their terms if they were not to struggle for a workforce. The work itself, at first anyway, was what the men were used to – clearing trees and rough ground, hedging and ditching, digging holes – but the more skilled tasks when the real building got underway needed more pairs of hands than the neighbourhood could provide. Over the next three years, Watton was something of a boom town, as the four great hangars went up and all the offices, quarters, messes and facilities were constructed for what was then considered a very modern station, with metalled apron in front of the hangars and a perimeter track, but no runways. Bomber aerodromes were still grass fields. There were no bombers big enough to need runways.

First unit there, February 1939, was 34 Squadron with the Blenheim Mark I; they would be off to Singapore in August. Next, 21 Squadron landed, also with the Mark I. For all personnel, especially those in the officers' mess, life was rather fine on such an up-to-date aerodrome. The countryside around Watton was excellent for riding and shooting, and dances in the mess became a considerable social attraction.

No. 82 came to Watton with the Mark IV on August 22, only

to be scattered nine days later to Horsham St Faith, thence to Netheravon on the day war was declared, to Bassingbourne, back to Horsham, and back to Bassingbourne. If an op were to be called, scattered aircraft would have to return to base to be armed, and crews to be briefed.

After the disastrous attack on German shipping in the Schillig Roads on 4 September, when five Blenheims of 107 and 110 Squadrons were lost for virtually no productive return, another attack was ordered for the 6th, to be made by 82 and 139 Squadrons. They stood ready all day. By late afternoon, they would have been wondering how they were supposed to find ships passing in the night. At six o'clock, the op was cancelled.

There were stand-bys most days after that, and from the 14th to the 16th, nine Blenheims of 82 and forty-five others stood by all day at three-quarters of an hour's notice, ready to attack the Kriegsmarine should it try to interfere with the Royal Navy's minelaying in the Channel. No call came, likewise when the squadrons moved to a more general readiness to combat German naval movements.

Hindsight is a wonderful thing, and we know that the RAF was not permitted to attack mainland Germany. The British and French governments had agreed to follow President Roosevelt's dictum that there were to be no civilian casualties, and Hitler had also concurred as soon as he had finished with Poland. This meant that the only legitimate target was warships at sea, but we have to ask why air force commanders thought it possible, never mind a good idea, to try to sink German battleships with Blenheims. Going in low meant that bombs would not penetrate and crews were very exposed to anti-aircraft fire from highly skilled and well-practised sailors. Later, orders would be given to other squadrons to attack from 10,000 feet, above the flak. It cannot have been considered relevant that, at that time with no accurate bombsight to work with, no RAF crew, in practice or in anger, in cloud or clear skies, had ever hit anything as small as a ship with a bomb from 10,000 feet, much less one that was steaming along taking evasive action.

Anyway, for 82 Squadron, ships became yesterday's priority. After Poland, a German invasion of France became a possibility and a new set of orders came in, for photo-reconnaissance of enemy communications – roads and railways – so that any subsequent build-up of forces could be measured, and of enemy airfields, twenty-eight of them, beginning on 27 September. Two Blenheims of 21 Squadron and three of 82 flew off to do this, with cameras not really suitable for the job. Flying Officer Hall of 82 came back with some marginally useful pictures taken above Hamburg and Fassburg. Pilot Officer Fordham saw the first real action for the squadron when he was attacked by flak near Wunsdorf and had to come down low, so low that he flew between two German aircraft, Heinkel 111s, which were on their landing approach. Fordham's WOp/AG fired on them but no effect was noted.

The third machine's captain, F/O Coutts-Wood, was an amateur photographer on the ground, Leica always in hand, but he suffered oxygen failure at 20,000 feet, turned south from Cologne towards France, got lost, and managed to find Auxerre aerodrome before running out of petrol.

Eventually, sixteen of the twenty-eight airfields were photographed, for the loss of two Blenheims of 110 Squadron. They found a complete lack of effective camouflage except at Fassburg, and the Luftwaffe had not followed the RAF's lead in dispersing aircraft to the boundaries but rather left them in their normal groupings. Had the Blenheims been attacking rather than photographing, they might well have had very good results.

Knowing that the ban on bombing Germany could not last, discussions now centred on enemy power stations, so photo-reconnaissance switched to those types of target as well as the constant look-out for signs of forces building up for an invasion of France. Indeed, there was a false alarm on 18 October, when a German offensive through Belgium was thought possible. If that had happened, 2 Group's Blenheims could have been there in response in four hours plus flying time. As it was, they could keep their machines on the ground so that the top brass's new idea, a fixed backward firing gun to be operated by the observer, could be fitted. Very few crews thought such armament would be any use at all. Of greater utility would be twin guns in the turret, but the trade-off in restricting the field of fire, especially to the rear where most fighter attacks could be expected, tipped the balance back to the single gun for the time being.

Still looking for improvements, a Blenheim of 139 Squadron was treated to a modest streamlining and polishing, resulting in a top-speed gain of 13mph, from 264mph to 277mph at 10,000 feet. This treatment was deemed too labour intensive/ expensive for everyone to have it but the first to get the treatment was also the first to have the new underside paint, colour 'light sea green', later known as duck-egg green. Squadrons were to have a few of these polished and painted machines for special missions.

No. 82 Squadron consolidated at Watton on 1 November 1939 and Group orders changed again soon after. Those solo reconnaissance flights had cost seven Blenheims, very nearly one loss in every five sorties. Ships were back on the list and there were many stand-bys that came to nothing, reconnaissance flights that depended entirely on the weather, plus a new coastal duty, which had the Group providing, on every third day, twenty-four Blenheims ready to go at two hours' notice. Christmas Eve, for example, had two aircraft of 82 Squadron looking for Deutschland class ships in port. These were the heavy cruisers that the British called pocket battleships,, the *Deutschland*, the *Admiral Scheer* and the *Admiral Graf Spee*, famously scuttled after the Battle of the River Plate. In any case, 82 Squadron didn't find them.

So far in the so-called Phoney War, up to the end of 1939, Bomber Command had lost sixty-eight aircraft in action and seventy-eight in non-operational crashes, mostly in training. Aircraft could be replaced; men learning their job, men teaching them, men lost in action who, at this time, were all experienced, pre-war regulars – these losses were harder to compensate for. Matters had been quieter at 82 Squadron, losing no machines in action and four Blenheims in training accidents with two fatalities, one crash being from a landing with the undercarriage up.

The plan for 2 Group had always been to remove to France,

to become part of the AASF (Advanced Air Striking Force), the optimistically named small collection of Blenheim and Fairey Battle squadrons. This had nothing to do with defending and repelling any German invasion of France, an event not considered likely when the plan was drawn up. Rather, the AASF's light bombers were meant to strike, and to strike into Germany from a more convenient distance should the enemy start bombing Britain. That this was an entirely mad idea must have occurred to almost everyone but it went ahead anyway.

The French thought differently, that the bigger the AASF, the less likely would be an invasion, but they never got around to building the aerodromes, so 2 Group stayed in Norfolk, Suffolk and Huntingdonshire. The Blenheims could still hit German targets but this looked less and less the way things would go. If the Germans decided to attack France via the Low Countries, the AASF would follow Plan B and become the defensive air-arm of the British Expeditionary Force, trying to stop an advance into France, and the home-based squadrons of 2 Group would be deployed in support. Some senior figures in the RAF believed that Blenheims and Battles would be of little use in stopping the Wehrmacht and would suffer huge losses in the process. Although it had been shown in several conflicts that bombers could be useful in support of an advancing army, there was no history of bombers trying to stop one.

The first real alarm came in January 1940. The Germans were planning an attack and 82 Squadron, along with 21, 107 and 110, were told on the 14th that they must get ready for a move to France. The invasion was expected on the 17th, and those four squadrons of Blenheims had better be prepared for some urgent and concentrated business. The warload would be 1,300lb of bombs, as two 250lb and the rest as twenty anti-personnel bombs, 40-pounders.

Individual skippers would decide on how to attack when they reached and saw the target, which would be an armoured column on a road or similar gathering; but there was something of a paradox in the orders. Going in above 1,000 feet would compromise accuracy; going in below that height would compromise the aircraft when its bombs went off.

Nothing happened on 17 January but it became increasingly clear that it was just the date the intelligence services had got wrong. The routes the enemy might take were mapped out, should he go for France directly with side thrusts into the Low Countries, or for France via Belgium, or for the whole lot starting at the top with The Netherlands. No. 82 at Watton and others had their instructions on 29 February: they were to cause traffic jams by bombing the leading troops and AFVs (Armoured Fighting Vehicles, or tanks) where the roads narrowed or there was some other opportune constriction.

The new year had blown in with a spell of atrocious weather that lasted past February. Fog, snow and rain meant that flying was much curtailed for No. 82. Squadron Leader Keeling came from the Air Ministry to give a talk: 'Hints on how to escape if taken prisoner'. Lieutenant Caldecote-Smith RN lectured on the German navy. When there was work that could be done, it was photo-reconnaissance, some to find the positions of flak ships. Orders from Group HQ: 'Two aircraft to take off to report on weather conditions East Anglia to vicinity of Heligoland. Avoid fighters by use of cloud etc.'

On another such trip came the squadron's first operational loss, 27 February, when a standard flight to the Heligoland Bight ended in a mystery. Orders: 'Two aircraft required to make recco and report on weather conditions also on salvage work on British submarines. Order of priority: (1) bring back a/c (2) weather recco (3) report on salvage operations.'

One of the crews was unable to meet their first priority. The body of F/O John Christopher Howell Blake, pilot, was found by the Germans. Those of Sergeant Thomas Sinclair Weightman, observer, aged 27, and AC1 Samuel Newton Middleton, WOp/AG, aged 19, never were.

Other squadrons' encounters with German fighters – Messerschmitt 110 and 109 – had already shown the Blenheim to be slow and vulnerable in comparison, with tight formation the best defence, but F/O Blake and crew were not in a formation. They were on their own. Operations Record Book (ORB): '12.30. Two aircraft took off on recco. 16.35. One aircraft returned from recco.' Leaving aside the German fighters, if they had tried to bomb a flak ship solo, the odds would have been heavily against them.

Then came the first definite blow inflicted on the enemy by No. 82. Squadron Leader (Acting Wing Commander) Miles 'Paddy' Delap, an Ulsterman from County Tyrone, with crew Corporal Allen Richards in the turret and observer Sgt Frank Wyness, were on a recco off Borkum on 11 March, looking at defences including barrage balloons. Descending to 4,000 feet they saw four brown balloons above the clouds. They came down to 1,000 feet and found a big surprise, a U-boat dawdling along on the surface. Delap dived into the attack, Wyness released their four bombs at once and they all saw two direct hits. The U-boat sank leaving only an oil slick but the aircraft had been damaged too, being so low over its own explosions. Delap had no idea at first what his unwelcome modifications were; he only knew that his Blenheim had acquired a tendency to fly in circles. Experienced pilot that he was, having qualified way back in 1928, he sorted things out and got them home. This is his DFC (Distinguished Flying Cross) citation, *London Gazette*, 2 April:

> During March, 1940, this officer was the pilot of an aircraft engaged in a reconnaissance flight over the Heligoland Bight. Whilst penetrating into a strongly defended area and descending through cloud to about 1,000 feet a submarine was sighted moving slowly on the surface. Squadron Leader Delap immediately attacked from about 500 feet allowing the submarine no time in which to submerge. He released a salvo of four bombs and two direct hits were observed. Squadron Leader Delap then continued the reconnaissance which produced valuable results.

Richards and Wyness were both awarded the other-ranks equivalent of the DFC, the DFM (Distinguished Flying Medal), but it was not announced until 17 May, something of a red-letter day in the squadron's history for altogether different reasons.

U–31 was the first U-boat sunk by the RAF. She was quite a famous vessel, having sunk nine Royal Navy and merchant ships with torpedoes and mines. All her crew of fifty-eight were lost but the Germans raised her, repaired and returned her to service to sink three more ships, to be herself sunk again in November by Royal Navy destroyer HMS *Antelope*, with most of the crew surviving, thus becoming the first U-boat to be sunk twice.

A satellite 'drome was built for Watton, down the road at Bodney, and the squadron removed there on 19 March, and matters in the war at large took a serious turn. German air attacks on the Royal Navy had had only modest success so far but, on the night of 17/18 March, five Heinkel 111s dive-bombed ships at Scapa Flow in the Orkney Islands. They damaged two, HMS *Norfolk* and HMS *Iron Duke*, killing four officers and wounding more. The rest of the formation went for an aerodrome nearby, with insignificant results except that bombs fell on a tiny village, Bridge of Wraith, killing one civilian and wounding seven more.

The dead man, James Isbister, a council worker, had been standing in his doorway watching the action. The Germans claimed the civilian casualties were caused by detritus from British anti-aircraft fire. The British claimed that fifty bombs and many incendiaries had fallen on land, wrecking several cottages, a car, and setting a farm building and straw stacks alight.

A gentlemanly response was devised, being an attack on the seaplane base at Hörnum, at the far southern end of the island of Sylt. It was a land target but, as stated, there were no civilians.

Fifty bombers went – thirty Whitleys, twenty Hampdens – of 50, 51, 61, 102 and 144 Squadrons, with six hours allocated between them for their bombing runs over the base. Forty-one of the attackers claimed to have found the target in clear weather, and to have hit it. Around twenty tons of general purpose bombs were dropped, plus 1,200 incendiaries, in the biggest job so far. One Whitley was lost, shot down by flak.

This was a first on many counts, including a technological first as the wireless operator in the leading aircraft was able to send coded messages reporting the attack, which started at 20.00, before it finished after 02.00, so that Mr Chamberlain could inform the House and the world that our bombers were hitting Germany, while the raid was still going on – 'an event probably without precedent in the history of warfare' as *The Times* had it.

Intelligence officers were delighted to hear about the accurate bombing, and 82 Squadron went to check early on the morning of the 20th. ORB: 'These two aircraft (Sutcliffe and Newbatt) made a photographic recco of Hornum to cover the area of the bombing raid night 19/3/40–20/3/40. Excellent photographs obtained despite intense A.A. fire.' Regrettably, the photographs showed little evidence of 41 bombers finding the target.

There were more routine recco flights while the Germans were assembling great numbers of ships in their northern ports, ready for what turned out to be their invasion of Denmark and Norway, although such routine was always laced with danger. Just how much the Germans didn't like being photographed was discovered by Sq/Ldr Walter

Sutcliffe, if he didn't know already, when he took pictures through especially concentrated flak over Sylt on 20 March. He had the DFC for that, added to his previous flights over the Heligoland Bight.

Attacking ships was not a very fruitful use of bombers. Success was rare and the bombing was dangerous; but when warships set sail they became legitimate targets. The embargo against hitting actual pieces of Germany, in case of civilian casualties, did not apply. The orders said seek and destroy, and nine of 82 took off from Bodney on 1 April to look for them off the Danish coast. Six machines turned back, frustrated by cloud and rain. One section of three couldn't find the warships either but just happened across two pairs of flak ships, two miles apart. Called by the Germans *Vorpostenboot*, outpost boat, these heavily armed conversions of small civilian ships, often fishing boats, were generally to be avoided if at all possible.

The section of three went in to bomb. No success was recorded for the attackers, but the defenders scored. ORB: 'No hits were observed, but some bombs seen to fall 50 yards short. F/O G Harries, Sgt H H Kelleway and AC E L Wolverson failed to return. It was not known what happened to this aircraft.' And that was despite the two others going back to the flak ships to search. It is not known either what happened to Harries, Kelleway and Wolverson, except that they were killed.

As one pilot put it, if you were flying alone in a Blenheim and met German fighters, you didn't come home, and if you didn't meet them, you were lucky. One 82 Squadron pilot proved another truth: flying was dangerous enough without meeting fighters. F/O Joe Hunt took off at dawn on 4 April to look for U-boats reported near Cuxhaven. The weather was awful, rain, cloud down almost to the sea, so he turned for home and the starboard engine stopped. Flying on one in a Blenheim was perfectly feasible, but Hunt lost his concentration and control of the aircraft when, in the middle of restarting his engine, he turned off the petrol supply. The machine dipped sharply back down towards the sea. Hunt got a grip again but not before he'd lost his tail wheel, snapped off in the water, and bent his starboard propellor. Like so many machines from the pre-computer age, the Blenheim had a great deal of built-in resilience and, even when severely handicapped, could be coaxed into performing by a skilled human. They climbed to safety and luckily not meeting the enemy, got home somehow.

This was remarkable for another reason. It was the second time he'd done it. Looking for an enemy naval patrol to attack, in similarly filthy weather, meant skimming the waves on 19 March. He dropped his bombs in a dive and managed to dip his tail wheel in the sea as he pulled out.

In a month of continuous stand-bys followed by nothing more than stand-downs, 4 April was a busy day, and all the work was concentrated on ships. 'Flying in rain at 250 feet … Very intense and accurate AA fire and tracer bullet machine-gun fire … Two ships probably of Scharnhorst/Gneisenau class observed, photos taken by gunner with Contax camera not successful owing to rain.' Well, at least he had a first-rate camera with him – German, of course, made by Zeiss Ikon of Dresden.

Another 82 Squadron crew saw the same ships and attacked with 250-pounders. 'Nearest bomb dropped 40 yards ahead.' Four destroyers were attacked by F/Lt George Watson: 'One bomb was a near miss,' and he had to fend off a Messerschmitt 110.

A few days later, 8 April, there were more fruitless ventures against shipping in northern waters, and a sergeant pilot called Bennett took a Blenheim up on a training flight with an extra man aboard, a student navigator. The aircraft emerged from cloud in a power dive about a mile from Bodney base above a field disguised as an aerodrome, a bombing decoy meant to lure the Germans away from Bodney and Watton, at Hollow Heath, Hilborough. Sgt Bennett baled out, too low to be safe, and was injured in the fall. His crew fared much worse, with no time to free themselves. Sgt Ian Murdoch, observer, age 22, MID (Mentioned in Despatches), was buried at home in Inverness. Sgt George Chapman, observer under training, was a 19-year-old lad from Invergordon, a dozen miles from Inverness as the Blenheim might fly. Frances and William, parents of AC2 John William Kempton, WOp/AG, 22, would receive their telegram at March in the Cambridgeshire fens.

Between 4 and 8 April, there were 45 Blenheim sorties flown looking for these ships. Of these, less than half found a ship and bombed it, but no crew recorded a hit.

Missing most of the previous base-hopping but arriving in time for Bodney and Watton – the squadron would be back there again on 1 May – was a new CO, and a most remarkable one. He was an Irish peer, the fifth Earl of Bandon, Percy Ronald Gardner Bernard, known to his many friends as Paddy.

In their youth, he and his twin brother went to the same schools, which must have been confusing for everyone. Paddy was officially known at Wellington College as Bernard Minor although he was the elder of the two by twenty minutes. Regardless of seniority, he was no great scholar, being much more inclined towards the rugby field and the running track. Sporting prowess had always been a good qualification for the armed forces but there was still the examination to pass if he was to be an officer, and that's what he wanted more than anything, in the Royal Air Force.

He was eighteen, it was 1922, and the RAF was struggling to survive political attacks from the army and navy, both of which considered a separate air force entirely unnecessary. Paddy was going to join it come what may; and so he spent his final summer holiday cramming on an intensive training course, which hard work got him through the entrance exams for the RAF College, Cranwell.

Officer Cadet Bernard became the fifth Earl of Bandon when a fairly remote relation died, the cousin of his grandfather. This was good news all round. Although there was a more or less bankrupt estate in County Cork, the IRA had burned the castle down so Paddy was pleased to receive the government compensation instead. The young Lord Bandon suddenly had the modern equivalent of about £6 million in the bank. He also didn't have the responsibility of a seat in the Lords, because it was an Irish peerage, but he did have that title, which was greatly pleasing to RAF senior management. The two other, more ancient services were quite used to having titled gentry in their ranks but it was a novelty for the newly born air force, and rather more important then than it would be now.

Paddy earned his wings and became an instructor for the rest of the 1920s, then had an overseas posting with 216 Squadron, originally a Royal Naval Air Service bomber unit but by this time flying mail and passengers between Empire stations in Africa and the Middle East. The passengers were usually troops, two dozen men sitting on the equivalent of camping stools, being flown to wherever trouble happened to be flaring up. The squadron was forging new routes all the time in some rather antiquated aircraft, including the Vickers Victoria. Paddy Bernard, now usually known as Paddy Bandon (sometimes lengthened to The Abandoned Earl), became the first pilot to fly non-stop from Khartoum to Cairo, about a thousand miles, which he achieved by his version of mid-air refuelling, from cans of petrol stored inside the aircraft.

He was a character, certainly, a notable practical joker who could swear as well as any trooper and who lacked something of the gravity that might have been expected in higher places. But he was a dashing pilot and an inspirational leader men would gladly follow.

It was typical of him and his attitude to life that a new posting, as a staff officer to the Anglo-French Supreme War Council, did not dismay him in the slightest even though he could speak no French. He simply arranged a swap with an old pal who could speak it but had been sent to the Directorate of Plans. Soon after that he joined Bomber Command 2 Group, also as a staff officer, and swiftly moved on to operational command with 82 Squadron in early 1940.

Wing Commander Bandon would retire as Air Chief Marshal GBE, CB, CVO, DSO. Meanwhile, he had a war to fight and, as one pilot put it: 'He was a fine morale booster, very loyal to the squadron and, in fact, he commanded affection and loyalty from everyone who met him.'

At the beginning of April 1940, the political tension could not have been higher, and not only about German plans for the Low Countries and France. Britain had been becoming increasingly furious with neutral Norway. Thousands of tons of (neutral) Swedish iron ore were being shipped from the Norwegian port of Narvik to Germany and thence down the ship-canal system to the industrial heartland, the Ruhr. The possibility of Britain invading Scandinavia had been put about by the German High Command for some time, to divert attention from their own campaign of espionage, intrigue and fifth-column work aided by the notorious Vidkun Quisling.

The Royal Navy laid mines inside Norwegian territorial waters in an attempt to stop the traffic. The Norwegian government issued a heated protest, threatening to declare war on Britain. The Allies jointly issued a list of sea areas into which Norwegian ships would sail at their peril.

The Germans were outraged, naturally. This was the most flagrant violation of neutrality ever seen. Added to which, the Allies were obviously too cowardly and weak to fight Germany directly, and so conducted an underhand war using the neutral countries as pawns in the game.

As the newspapers published the Allies' list of forbidden sea areas on the morning of 9 April, Germany simultaneously invaded Norway and Denmark. By the time British readers had moved on to the crossword and the latest advice from Lord Woolton to housewives, Denmark had decided that the better part of valour was discretion, and was occupied. The southern half of Norway followed after a stiff but short fight.

Such action was deeply regretted by Germany. It was only important military objectives that were the concern, and it was all done to secure Scandinavia against Allied aggression. Germany would respect the freedom and independence of the peoples of Denmark and Norway, and hoped very much that such respect would not be prejudiced by anything as silly as resistance, passive or active.

The Germans' real purpose was more complex than simply securing the iron ore. They did indeed want to prevent the Allies from setting up bases in Norway from which to attack northern Germany, and they wanted naval bases – especially U-boat pens – and aerodromes to give them better access to their enemy's shipping lanes. Above all, they wanted to test just how determined and competent the Allies would be in a total war.

The orders came in from Group, telling 82 Squadron to get ready to sink ships, then telling them not to bother. Nobody had ever severely damaged a surface warship at sea with a bomb, much less sunk one, but every day the squadron stood by to do the impossible, then stood down.

Notification came to Bodney on 14 April that invasion of the Low Countries was imminent, so 82 was to be sent to recco the probable routes of the advance. There were four routes, with two aircraft assigned to each. 'Recco can only be completed successfully by flying at low altitude. Obtain photos if possible. Do not carry bombs. Avoid AA defences at Wesel, Rheine and Münster.'

This was serious stuff to set the nerves a-jangle. Flying low over Germany, looking for armoured columns – that would make a change from Heligoland. Of course, the Germans didn't invade and the orders switched back to warships in the blessed Schillig Roads, Wilhelmshaven and everywhere else around the Bight where they hardly ever saw anything to bomb.

On the 9th, a single platoon of German paratroops had captured Ålborg aerodrome, the Danes making no effort to stop them, in the first action of its kind in the history of warfare. Danish airfields would be highly convenient for air-raids on the UK; dusk attacks were to be made on Ålborg and Rye aerodromes, 'to light fires for the benefit of the night bombers', which would cause 'maximum disorganisation and damage'. Crews were to be warned that if they flew low and fast they would run short of petrol and, curiously, they were told to 'aim incendiaries at the target. It is most important that they fall on aerodrome. Release of bombs by judgement on run-up.' Whatever the crews might have thought of such statements of the obvious, it didn't matter. They didn't go. Orders cancelled again.

Thus, in April 1940, Germany had subdued Denmark and Norway with a minimum of effort, and Poland before that. When Hitler turned his gaze to the west, which way would he come? The French believed they could withstand any attack on their defensive barrier, the famous Maginot Line. So smashed up would the Germans be, that attack would turn swiftly into ignominious retreat.

Since the Germans knew the strength of the Maginot Line as well as anyone, said the doubters, why would they try to break it when there was a much easier route through The Netherlands and Belgium? Belgium was neutral but so she had been in 1914 and that hadn't bothered the Germans in the slightest. Denmark had been neutral a few days ago.

The Dutch did believe themselves to be at great risk. Their forces were ready, determined, not so well armed, a gallant few – alas no match for the mighty Wehrmacht and Luftwaffe. The Belgians did have defences, but they would be badly exposed if The Netherlands fell, and there were no defences to speak of between Belgium and France, and none in Luxembourg.

The British sent aircraft from their France-based squadrons of Battles and Blenheims to recco possible airfields in advanced positions, so they could move up there to face the invaders more closely.

Meanwhile, the Allies could not decide whether, in the event of a German invasion, they should hold the line at the French border or, assuming the attack had been halted by Dutch and/or Belgians, advance through the Low Countries and meet the Germans head on.

CHAPTER THREE

THE WAR IN NORFOLK

Who live under the shadow of a war,
What can I do that matters?

Stephen Spender might have written those words for the boys of 82 Squadron, keen to get into the action but so far seeing war according to an earlier definition, as long periods of boredom punctuated by moments of terror, except the punctuations hadn't really happened.

On the first day of the month of May, 82 swapped bases, Bodney for Watton, with 21 Squadron, and had six aircraft and crews standing by (again) for an attack on Ålborg aerodrome (again). Many moments of terror would occur at Ålborg later in the year but for now (and again) the op was cancelled. Never mind, twelve machines were bombed up and stood by at one hour's notice, only to be stood down at 21.30. Bombing up with a mixed load of 40-pounder anti-personnel bombs and 250lb general-purpose bombs was a time-consuming business but the armourers got on with it, and debombed when yet another stand down came, and bombed up again for another stand-by, one hour's notice from 05.30 next morning. Two sections stood down at 15.30, one to stay on an hour's notice, another on three hours, all sections stood down at 20.00.

From 2 May, the Blenheims of 2 Group were withdrawn from Scandinavian duty as a German attack to the west and south was believed imminent. The result, for a few days at any rate, was just another sort of stand-by. Here is Blenheim WOp/AG Richard Passmore:

> We stood by until light was fading and were then told we might stand down until the following day. Relieved, we went off to tea. That evening we listened more intently than usual to the news bulletins; they were clearly as confused as our intelligence reports had been. We knew that sooner or later our people would find targets for us and that we should then be sent in, time and time again, to do what we could. It was not a pleasant thought to sleep on, but none of us seemed to have much difficulty in going to sleep.

When would they be doing something that mattered? Maybe 82's Flight Lieutenant George Hall would have better luck, promoted to Squadron Leader and posted to 110 Squadron in Lossiemouth where, doubtless, even with his new responsibilities, he would be repeating his party trick of falling backwards to the floor with a drink in his hand.

Stand by, stand down, stand by, stand down – long periods of boredom for aircrew, punctuated not by terror but by lectures on 'First Aid in the Air' and 'Administration of Oxygen'. The armourers took the opportunity of fitting the observer-fired, rear-firing gun under the noses of those machines yet to be so fitted. Maybe that would come in handy when the balloon went up, or not. Bombing practice was the usual shallow diving at moderate heights, and experiments with a new low-level bombsight seemed promising.

If you were one of the few crews not on stand-by, you might have blind take-off practice, or a trip to Mildenhall to practise Lorenz approaches. The Lorenz system was a German method for landing blind, adopted by the RAF, which worked on a radio signal. The receiver in the cockpit gave out a series of beeps – dots if you were off line to port, dashes if to starboard, and a continuous tone if you were right on the mark.

There were cross-country flights too, to keep the navigators up to speed, and all this was still happening on 9 May. Next day it was different – in a way. As the Germans began the Blitzkrieg, all of 82 Squadron's aircraft and crews were on one-hour stand-by and so, as the Recorder of Operations observed, 'no training flying could be carried out'.

Stand-down came at 16.00, but they were on an hour's notice again from 03.30, 11 May. Orders came in three more times that day but none led to an op. The situation was fluid to say the least – the Germans were here, or nearly there, or already past that point. Targets could not be assigned with any certainty and aircrew, eager for action, found the delays and confusion very wearing indeed on the nerves, and imagined that situation to be worse than the reality of attacking the enemy.

Meanwhile, another set of orders came from HQ, telling 82 and two other squadrons to be ready to move to France.

The orders were written before the German attack but in expectation of it. The 'probable role of the squadrons will be, during the very early stages after the violation of Holland, to reconnoitre to locate the advance of enemy columns, and to attack columns of AFVs and mechanised columns at the head of the advancing armies'.

No mention here of the possibility of paratroops taking airfields, as they had done in Norway and Denmark. In any event, while the top brass was not deciding where to make a stand, and the staff officers of 2 Group were sending out their travel warrants, the Germans had struck simultaneously at several points on the Dutch and Belgian borders, in much greater force than had been expected. Paratroops took the Dutch airfields long before mechanised columns could have reached them, and air support and ground forces swept in behind.

Suddenly, 2 Group's priorities were bridges over rivers and canals, and those now-enemy aerodromes, as a force given over to Air Marshal Sir Arthur 'Ugly' Barrett and his command, the AASF. Still, matters were no clearer at Watton. There was more standing by on 12 May, more stand-downs and more bombing up, finishing with nine machines ready to go at 16.00, and at 19.00, glory be, they were ordered into the air. They circled, and at 19.30 they set off for the target, a road bridge over the Albert Canal north of Hasselt in The Netherlands.

They were too late. Airborne troops had already overcome fierce Belgian resistance to take Fort Eben-Emael by landing on its roof, an exercise rehearsed in the strictest secrecy since the very beginnings of the war, and were in complete charge of the three bridges that the fort's guns overlooked. By the time the 82 boys got their final instructions, the Germans had been in possession for a full day and more, plenty of time to set up their phenomenally good anti-aircraft batteries.

There are no records of what happened to those nine crews after 19.30. We know there were no losses, likewise no story of success or failure. Perhaps they were recalled. Perhaps, luckily for them, they never got to Hasselt.

Elsewhere it was a much bloodier story. The AASF was striking all right, but it was also being struck at an horrific rate. In a disastrous attack on the Albert Canal, 12 Squadron won two posthumous VCs but lost five Fairey Battles. By the evening of 12 May, Day Three of the Blitzkrieg, half of the AASF had disappeared. 'Ugly' Barrett said his force of 135 machines at the start of Day One had been reduced by 63 to 72. It was worse than that if you counted those aircraft that got home but were so badly shot up that they'd never fly again. There were also some destroyed on the ground by German bombers that Barrett may not have known about yet, and in fact the total was the other way around, more like 72 lost leaving 63, all Blenheims and Battles. The fighters also had losses, ten or more Hurricanes.

Flying from UK, 2 Group lost a further nineteen Blenheims trying to stop the Wehrmacht, including six – plus one beyond repair – in a single raid by 15 Squadron, and four of 107 Squadron following in to the same target. *The Luftwaffe War Diaries* describes this, a great event from their point of view, and a clear demonstration of the Me109's superiority over the Blenheim:

At 06.00 First Lieutenant Walter Adolph observed some dark dots in the lightening sky to the east. Three, six, nine of them. They grew larger; too large to be fighters … twin engined bombers, coming rapidly nearer. Red, white, blue roundels … English … type Bristol Blenheim. A hundred yards astern of the last of them Adolph went down, then coming up again approached obliquely from below. The bombers stuck rigidly to their course. Hadn't they noticed anything?

In his reflector sight the Blenheim appeared as big as a haystack. He glanced momentarily to the left, saw Sergeant Blazytko closing with the next bomber, and pressed the button. Cannon and machine-guns went off together at a range of eighty yards, and little flashes dotted the target's fuselage and wings. Adolph threw his plane in a turn to avoid colliding, and looking back saw the Blenheim's port engine on fire. Suddenly the whole wing broke off. The rest of the plane seemed to stop. Then, rearing up, it went down to destruction.

Adolph at once went after another Blenheim, and within five minutes had shot down three. Three more were claimed … as if that were not enough, the remaining three were spotted during their escape over Liège … two of them crashed to the ground in flames.

Unusually for such reports, the losses were worse than the fighter pilot described but not all the victories were due to fighters. Twelve Blenheims of 15 Squadron took off at dawn for the Albert Canal bridges at Maastricht, with the standard orders to stick together in formation unless forced apart by intense flak. Six were shot down in the target area with fourteen crewmen dead and four taken prisoner, and one more aircraft was so badly beaten up that it never flew again. The Blenheims 'spotted during their escape' were part of the follow-up raid by 107 Squadron, with three shot down, one force-landed in the Liège area, and another struggling home to a no-wheels belly-flop.

As 82 Squadron would be in a few days' time, the twelve of 107 Squadron were flying in two boxes of six. F/O Gareth Clayton DFC, later the belly-flopper, was leading the second box: 'I closed in hard behind and just below Embry's leading box [Wing Commander Basil Embry DSO and Bar, AFC, later to evade capture in amazing fashion after being shot down over Dunkirk] making it a tight formation of twelve, flying in on the bomb run, but this did not last for long. Ahead of us I could see exploding AA fire – as well as being a good bombing height, 6,000 feet was also perfect for the Germans' excellent 88mm gun.'

The pilot of the force-landed machine was F/O Ronald Rotheram: 'As we approached the bridges at Maastricht, I could see intense flak as another formation attacked the bridges ahead of us. My aircraft was hit repeatedly and Sergeant Brown (observer) was wounded in his arm. Controls to the port engine were severed and the starboard engine damaged.'

Rotheram carried on to bomb, only to find two Me109s in hot pursuit. Escape in a small amount of cloud was followed by his port prop falling off and a crash landing in unoccupied Belgium.

Eleven of the twelve of 107 Squadron were hit by flak as they went in to the target, one fatally. The flak forced a break-up of the formation; although some were able to reform as a group in defence against the fighters following them out of the target area, and one Me109 was claimed shot down, Blenheims v Messerschmitts was not a fair fight, a fact which all Blenheim crews were surely well aware of by now.

Nothing much happened on the 13th in Bomber Command. There was a small op by the AASF aimed at the roads near Breda. A hit was claimed on a crossing and one Battle went down, nobody killed, while 82 Squadron was ordered, not to stand by, but to 'stand to, a condition difficult to define' according to the Recorder of Operations, on a day for licking wounds and taking stock. At Watton, a few of the observers went up for flying instruction. Perhaps there was speculation in the mess afterwards about the chances of an observer scrambling up from his cramped position to take over flying the aircraft with a dead or wounded pilot in a low-level attack, which was the kind they were expecting to make.

Expectation became reality the next day, 14 May, and six of 82 Squadron flew from Watton, take-off time of Paddy Delap in the lead at 11.21, having been standing by since 04.00. The target was a crossroads between Breda and Tilburg. Breda, a strategically important Dutch town not far from the Belgian border, was also a target for large forces of Germans thrusting into The Netherlands from the east, and the mayor of Breda had been instructed by the French commander to evacuate. French forces intended to make a stand around Breda and Tilburg and turn the tide of war against the Germans there, and by 14 May that should have happened, except they had left Tilburg to the Germans, who had also crossed the river into Breda - the CO of the Dutch forces in Brabant and all his staff officers were POWs.

The French had retreated towards Antwerp on 13 May and the defensive line was now west of Breda, the road to Roosendaal, along which crowds of refugees from evacuated Breda were trying to make their way, often under fire from the Luftwaffe. Such up-to-date information was not available to the RAF and those six of 82 Squadron set off 'with the intention of blocking' the Breda–Tilburg road, which was a little like shutting the stable door after the cavalry regiments had bolted. That the road was not already blocked with retreating wrecks of French armour was a credit to the hard scrap-metal work of the German infantry.

The squadron went in at their particular crossroads with the Germans well settled in their positions. Bombs dropped from between 5,000 and 2,000 feet hit the roadway, some houses around, and the Breda–Tilburg railway line, crews all the while under heavy anti-aircraft fire. According to the men coming home, the ack-ack gunners seemed to have got their height worked out especially well. The standard tactic of shallow dives would allow gunners the opportunity to make better calculations, but flying in close line astern, as these boys did, meant they were in and out before the gunners could focus on any one of them.

All the 82 Squadron men did get home and, amazingly, could tell the ground crews that each machine was being returned in perfect condition. Six crews, eighteen men, safely delivered from fatal dangers on Tuesday, back in time for lunch at around 13.55, and every one of them fated to experience terror and destruction on Friday.

The Germans had reached the River Meuse near Sedan in a spearhead attack, while the French 9th Army had obligingly vacated the Sedan area and moved north to confront the Germans in Belgium. The Luftwaffe had flown 500 bombing sorties in the late afternoon, well in front of their ground forces, keeping the French artillery quiet and stopping any attempts at reinforcement. Huge numbers of the German military could be seen moving unhindered to support the spearhead, and their 1st Rifle Regiment was over the river.

Any cold analysis of air-war potential would have considered the situation hopeless, but retreat was not yet an option for the RAF. Every available Battle was sent, with the last functioning French-based Blenheim squadron, No. 139, against the Sedan bridgehead and, in the evening, more 2 Group Blenheims, including eleven of 21 Squadron, flying from Bodney. They left around 18.00 with various targets assigned, of troops in woods, bridges, armoured columns, all in the Sedan area. One machine and its crew was lost without trace. Another crashed in Belgium after a fight with several Me109s; the crew managed to get back home. The third belly-flopped into Bodney, shot up beyond repair but claiming a Me109 downed. The news back at base was that The Netherlands' capitulation had been announced on Dutch wireless at 18.40.

It was named 'the day of the fighters' by the Luftwaffe, but 14 May was the day of the flak gunners too, if all the figures were to be believed. The fighters flew over 800 sorties and claimed 179 Allied aircraft shot down; the gunners claimed another 112. These 291, had they been real, would have had to have been mostly French as the Dutch air force hardly existed at the start of the day, down to about 30 machines of which only 10 were fighters, and the AASF had less than 70.

Bomber Command actual losses for the day were forty-seven, all but nine being AASF, almost exactly half of the sorties flown and more or less half of the already-halved AASF. No such losses had ever been imagined, much less seen before, nor would a proportion like that occur again in a sizeable operation – but then, never again would such an imbalance be struck between huge numbers of modern fighters against so many unsuitable, vulnerable bombers flying low over anti-aircraft batteries.

Some of the men who had been to Breda joined up with a large quota of the rest of 82 Squadron next day, 15 May, led by the great Paddy Bandon with LAC Freddie Thripp in the turret (of whom more later). Twelve of them took off from Watton around 13.30. The target was troop concentrations at the little French town of Monthermé, population then just short of 4,000, nowadays a tourist attraction for its ancient abbey and church and its picturesque position inside a broad meander of the Meuse where it meets the river Semoy, surrounded by the Ardennes forests. This is the very north-east of France, close to the Belgian border, just a few kilometres north of Charleville-Mézières and Sedan and not all that far from the squadron's Great War flying grounds of the Aisne.

There was fighter cover from the French air force, Hawk H75 aircraft, the Armée de l'Air version of the American

Curtiss P-36, which, like the Blenheims they were defending, had been considered the epitome of aerial technology when it first appeared in 1935 but was now outgunned, outpaced and outclimbed by the Me109.

Paddy and his men didn't meet any Messerschmitts at first but, as was the case on all these low-flying missions, they ran into heavy ground fire. They were employing the same shallow-dive tactic that was meant to reduce the chances of an anti-aircraft hit, and it worked again. They split from their sections of three and dive-bombed in line astern, which seemed not to suit the German gunners who managed only two superficial hits.

In the town square were massed many enemy vehicles and these were bombed, as were the houses beside the road leading to the river; the road was filled with rubble and rendered impassable for the time being. A good day was almost made excellent when a 109 came up on the port quarter of the Blenheim flown by F/Lt Charlie Breese, fired, and was sent away wounded in the wing by WOp/AG Corporal I T Harris. A single Me110 was also spotted but it stood off, while the somewhat braver crew of a Henschel 126 had a go. This machine was a slow, high-wing, general-purpose reconnaissance aircraft, looking something like the Westland Lysander that became famous for ferrying SOE parachutists into occupied France later in the war. The Henschel came in with its fixed machine gun firing forwards and its second gun operated by the observer in his open cockpit, attacking two Blenheims, which fired back with no result to either side.

So, 36 men of 82 Squadron flew home in time for tea.

Eleven of those at Monthermé would live to fight another day. The rest would live longer.

Their raid was quickly followed up by four AASF Blenheims of 139 Squadron, a remarkable feat in itself as they had lost four the day before and seven two days before that. The fighters were up in strength by now, to shoot down one Blenheim and damage the others, and among all this chaos the Air Ministry issued a statement:

> In the fury of these engagements [in the Sedan area] detailed reports from aircraft crews cannot be expected. Heavy losses must be suffered in attacking vital objectives which are strongly defended by anti-aircraft fire and enemy fighters.
>
> Our losses, which are not considered excessive in view of the results obtained, were 35 aircraft. Several crews from these aircraft, however, have already returned to their aerodromes.

The Ministry might have added that detailed reports on enemy movements from soldiers at the Front also could not be expected, although aircraft crews had to fly whatever the quality of their information. What they had was almost always out of date, and briefings were skimpy – here's a list of roads, you might find what you're looking for on them. Crews had some faith in the results obtained but really they were no more than a local nuisance to the Germans, a temporary inconvenience. As for the 'not excessive' losses – Air Marshal Barratt knew very well what that meant, as his force was halved every couple of days until he decided he could no longer send brave men in inadequate machines to their destruction in daylight. That was mainly Fairey Battles, of course. Barratt had virtually no Blenheims left, but 2 Group still had plenty to throw into the boiling pot and 82 Squadron was encouraged by messages of congratulation from the chiefs of the French forces.

Four crews of 82 were delegated to help out with AASF reinforcements. More machines from Fighter Command were urgently needed but Hurricane pilots could not be expected to find their way across France so, next day, an expedition of Blenheims led by Sq/Ldr Walter Sutcliffe flew to Manston and from there escorted twelve Hurricanes to Merville and other aerodromes. Among the boys on this little French holiday, unlikely to meet any Germans that far from the front line, were the gunning master of Monthermé, Corporal Harris, a nineteen-year-old WOp/AG called Thripp, six more from the Monthermé op and four others who had no idea just how fortunate they were. Six more crews were stood by from 04.00 to attack troops but they didn't have to go.

If 82 Squadron had had some luck to ride so far, that was the last of it. That night of the 16th/17th, on stand-by as usual, the aircrews went to bed while the ground crews worked on, urgently trying to keep as many aircraft serviceable as they possibly could. Those men had no reason to fear the dawn, but the pilots, navigators and WOp/AGs never knew what the day would bring. For twenty-two of them, the dawn of 17 May 1940 would be the last they'd ever see, and another three would not see Watton again in wartime.

CHAPTER FOUR

'WHERE'S EVERYBODY ELSE, MORRISON?'

By the evening of 15 May, the German panzer corps were over the river Meuse and cutting across northern France like the proverbial hot knife through butter. Guderian and Rommel, panzer commanders, were expecting to continue their advance west, right up to the Channel coast, thus cutting off the Allied armies to the north, including the BEF. It is said that Hitler was so deeply impressed by the ease and speed of this victory that he began to think he'd won too much too soon, and the fight now taking place at Gembloux must have reinforced those worries.

With no notion of the Germans' plan to make this thrust at Sedan, the French strategy had been for a pitched battle further north, to stop the enemy getting into central Belgium. A low ridge across the Belgian plain, the Gembloux Gap, would be ideal tank territory and so plans were made for a major defensive action near the small towns of Gembloux and

Hannut. The Germans were at Hannut by 12 May, Day Three of the invasion, and the French sent a strong armoured force to meet them with the brief to hold out long enough for the French First Army to dig in and get ready. The preparatory defensive works expected from the Belgians had hardly been started, never mind completed.

Hannut turned into a tank battle, with the French scoring some successes but, by its location it gave the Germans more freedom to advance at Sedan. The French fell back to Gembloux, again with both sides gaining and losing, but this time it was the Germans who were tied up. Try as they might, they could not force the breakthrough, though the French were suffering irreparable damage in the meantime.

Both sides had huge numbers of casualties, in men and machines, and neither could claim victory. This was a highly confused situation. After counter-attacks by the French Moroccans on the night of the 15th and the British Second Infantry Division on the 16th, the Germans and the French both implemented a strategic withdrawal. This part of the Blitzkrieg was halted, temporarily, but it would prove to be long enough to frustrate the encircling strategy of the Wehrmacht, the Sickle Plan, and eventually allow the great evacuation at Dunkirk.

Come the morning of 17 May, the AASF had at Barratt's disposal a dozen Hurricanes, six Blenheims and forty-five Battles in various states of readiness, but he wasn't going to send any more Battles in daylight. He could not hope to achieve anything but suicide with six Blenheims against two Divisions of panzers and three of infantry, including their numerous and efficient anti-aircraft units, reinforced by flocks of Luftwaffe fighters, so he didn't try. His only AASF losses that morning were four Fairey Battles left behind on the ground, as 88 and 142 Squadrons withdrew further into France. There would be more losses in the afternoon and evening, when Blenheims of the army's Air Component made reconnaissance flights and bombed columns of troops, but that was later. Before that, at dawn in Watton, 2 Group's greatest disaster of the war – so far – was about to begin.

With a historic view, we might ask what were Barratt's hopes for twelve Blenheims flying from England against those same German forces at Gembloux? The daylight was just as bright wherever you came from and whatever inadequate aircraft you were in. He knew what had happened to his AASF Blenheims – thirty of them lost, and thirty more down of 2 Group flying from England – but that's what he ordered, the only operation of the morning, twelve Blenheims of 82 Squadron to attack the German Sixth Army. Having withdrawn from the battle of the Gembloux Gap, while their French opponents were retreating over the border towards Lille, this formidable force was hurt enough not to want another day of battle on the ground but was not otherwise engaged. Their anti-aircraft gunners had had very little to do during the battle, against an almost non-existent air threat from the French, while the Luftwaffe had enjoyed complete air superiority. There had been 500-plus fighters at the disposal of German commanders on 10 May. If the number had been at all depleted, that was more than made up by reinforcements on the 15th.

There was no organised Allied defence now in central

Belgium. The Front, as it were, had disappeared and the Germans could more or less walk across after a day or two's rest, but Allied confusion and poor information led to a panic about a breakthrough, needing an urgent response. From whom, Barratt might have asked, and with what?

Breakthrough? It was a resolved matter. The main thrust towards Gembloux, a working town of around 5,000 inhabitants, had come from the Namur direction, from the south east, and along that road were now deployed two Divisions, one motorised, one infantry, with all the attendant weaponry to defend against air attack. Many of the inhabitants had gone, fleeing west. The German troops, tanks and ack-ack had taken over and moved west, too, beyond Gembloux, north of Charleroi.

Over in Norfolk, twelve Blenheim crews were told at 04.00 that they were on an hour's notice and, almost simultaneously, that the notice was here, to fly to a certain crossing, a bottleneck – a defile in military terms – on the Namur–Gembloux road. It is said that they were promised fighter escorts, surely a necessity on such a raid. Some of the men at the briefing knew from experience that such promises were sometimes kept.

All of them were RAF regulars from before the war. There were several twenty-year-olds among the WOp/AGs, but some of the older pilots and observers had seen great changes in a very few years: George Watson, for example, Flight Lieutenant, twenty-six, pilot, married to June; his observer Frank Wootten also twenty-six; and WOp/AG Alf Sims, twenty-five and with a wife called May – quite an elderly crew really, compared to the usual profile later in the war. In their flying careers they had seen bomber aircraft double and triple their air speed, and biplane fighters like the Hawker Fury, first in the RAF to go over 200mph, superseded by Spitfire and Hurricane at well over 300mph, which was just as well if they were to protect the Blenheims against the Messerschmitt 109.

At 04.15, the twelve were led into the air by Paddy Delap, with observer Sgt Frank Wyness and, in the turret, P/O Frank Jackson. While they were away, the *London Gazette* would announce the DFC for Delap, DFM for Wyness and DFM for Cpl Allen Richards, for their sinking of the U-boat. Richards was with F/O Fordham on this one, the first 82 Squadron captain to see flak and to fire on a German aircraft, back in September 1939.

They had a simple route – out over Felixstowe, across the Belgian coast between Ostend and Zeebrugge, check pinpoint at the town of Fleurus, then the last few miles to the target. Felixstowe was a quiet little holiday resort in those days; the weather was nice enough on the day to tempt a few onto the beach, or along the prom and the pier.

If the boys expected to rendezvous with fighters somewhere along the line, they were disappointed. There were no Hurricanes, no Spitfires. Perhaps there had been a slight cock-up in the communications department. Clear skies forecast over Belgium; they could already see that the forecast was spot on. Never mind, the blast of war was blowing in their ears, sinews were stiffened, blood summoned up, and it was six o'clock on a glorious morning, approaching the target with a few minutes to go, when they saw the first evidence of the enemy, a burst of flak a couple of miles away, low, no threat.

Moments later they flew right into a new ack-ack barrage, one of high intensity and great accuracy, fired from an emplacement near Nivelles, about 20 miles west of Gembloux. Immediately, one of the first shells hit UX/T, Bob McConnell's machine, right in the bomb-bay among the 40-pounders, the anti-personnel bombs, and set the aircraft on fire. Operations Record Book Appendix report: 'At 06.03 hours, A.A. fire began on our level. It was very accurate, the first shell hitting No. 2 in the No. 1 formation, making him go down.'

The pilot turned south and away from that small box of sky filled with horror but the damage was done. They were losing height, flames everywhere, explosion far more likely than a crash landing. They had managed about 10 miles in a shallow dive, smoke pouring forth, and were just north of Charleroi, away from the fighters and not quite finished yet.

ORB: 'Ack-ack was encountered before reaching the objective and the Squadron opened up and took evasive action.'

While McConnell was realising that his war appeared to be over, the rest of the formation split up, as they were drilled to do under this sort of anti-aircraft fire, when there was no apparent space between the shells screaming up, and climbed from 7,500 feet to 9,000. There was still a target to attack and they were almost on it. Just at that moment, the conductor of ack-ack batteries waved his baton and the shooting stopped. Why? Because he didn't want to hit any of his own aircraft.

To the east on the far side of Gembloux, a flock of Messerschmitt 109s was ready to pounce, ready to come down like wolves on the fold. *'For the Angel of Death spread his wings on the blast, And breathed in the face of the foe as he pass'd.'* Lord Byron was describing Assyrians in chariots but the image applies.

Delap saw them coming and ordered his men to close up into formation and head south, a right-angle turn, but there was no time. The Germans attacked with the sun behind them and with practised precision, in groups of three in line astern. Each deadly team aimed for one of the rearmost Blenheims and the fighter pilots took turns to hit it with cannon and machine gun as they soared past.

Delap's machine was hit but carried on. Among the first to go down, exploding in a mass of flames, was Alex Gofton's UX/R. He'd been at Monthermé with the same crew, observer Fred Miller, married man, and young Tom, Corporal Cummins, twenty years old, in the turret. No trace of them or their aircraft would ever be discovered.

UX/D was captained by Reg Newbatt, twenty-two, mentioned in despatches for photography under fire over Sylt. Both crew members were older but none of the three, all sergeants, was married. Joe Crawley, observer, was from St Helens, and Bert Knowles, twenty-five, was from Liverpool. Nothing of them or their aircraft was ever found – at least, nothing identifiable. Unknown airman in unmarked grave was sometimes the fate of flyers like these.

In this first wave of fighter attacks, one of the survivors, LAC M C Cleary, Jock Morrison's WOp/AG, reckoned he saw three or four Blenheims go down in flames. We now know there were four and they were Gofton, Newbatt, Toft and Christensen. Glaswegian P/O Severin Christensen, only twenty-one, and his crew – Alf Phillips and Peter Ettershank – and aircraft UX/Y disappeared entirely from the face of the earth.

Pilot Officer Ken Toft scrambled out of his aircraft as it made its fatal dive and he would be taken prisoner; but Arthur Crouch, married to Lilian, and Raymonde Morris, a Romford boy – if they were not already dead, they were certainly killed in the mid-air explosion and there was nothing left of them to be found.

After their first swoop, the fighters climbed away to sort themselves back into their sections, which gave the remaining seven Blenheim crews a brief respite. They headed south-west as fast as they could go, perhaps hoping that the Messerschmitts had run out of ammo, or perhaps praying for a miracle.

There was no miracle likely in Delap's machine. With the first attack over, the WOp/AG, Frank Jackson, married to Kathleen and twenty-two years old, called on the intercom to say he had been badly wounded. Delap ordered 'stand by', which meant 'get your parachutes on'.

The top speed of a fully loaded Blenheim was around 220/230mph. A few days before, on 4 May 1940, the Royal Aircraft Establishment had been running tests on a captured Me109 E series, which was the type flown by the pilots now eyeing up the remains of 82 Squadron. Here are some of the comments made:

> During a dive at 400mph all three controls were in
> turn displaced slightly and released. No vibration,
> flutter or snaking developed. As speed is increased,

the ailerons become heavier, but response remains excellent. They are at their best between 150mph and 200mph, one pilot describing them as an 'ideal control' over this range. Above 200mph they start becoming unpleasantly heavy, and between 300mph and 400mph are termed 'solid' by the test pilots. A pilot exerting all his strength cannot apply more than one-fifth aileron at 400mph. Good Points: High top speed and excellent rate of climb. Engine does not cut immediately under negative 'g'. Good control at low speeds. Bad Points: Ailerons and elevator far too heavy at high speeds. Owing to high wing loading the airplane stalls readily under 'g' and has a relatively poor turning circle. Cockpit too cramped for comfort.

A later conclusion was: 'There is no doubt that in 1940 the Bf.109E, in spite of its faults, was a doughty opponent to set against our own equipment.' What was meant by 'our own equipment' was the Spitfire and the Hurricane. Despite their poor turning circle and heavy controls at 400mph, fifteen examples of the E Series were more than doughty when set against seven Bristol Blenheims.

The Blenheims were still bombed up. They had not reached the target, had not dropped their loads in anger, and skippers would not willingly jettison over what was still friendly territory.

For McConnell, it was time to go. He couldn't keep his machine in the air any longer. They were a few miles north-east of Hirson, near the French border. Observer Sgt S J Fulbrook went out of the front hatch while the pilot was struggling to get his own hatch open. The WOp/AG, LAC H Humphreys, also managed to get out but he had been wounded.

Sgt Fulbrook, observer in that one aircraft to be downed by ground-fire, later made a report to Paddy Bandon: 'My last sight of the pilot was him attempting to open the top hatch of the aircraft. I went out of the front gun hatch and my parachute took a long time to open. On my way down I was shot at by some French soldiers, who took me for a Hun parachutist. I landed in some woods about 12 kilometres east of Couvin.' He was about 40 miles south-east of Nivelles where they'd taken the hit.

Fulbrook's reluctant parachute saved him in more ways than one. The pilot, McConnell, either landed in enemy-held territory or strayed into it and was taken prisoner.

By this time, approximately 06.20, the remaining seven were in the Hirson/St Quentin/Laon area, heading into France as far and as fast as possible. The fighters came in for their second spree, from the starboard quarter, and picked on UX/B, captain Sgt T J Watkins. The pilot heard his gunner, Ken Reed, blasting away but not for long. The port engine was on fire and clearly they'd had it. Watkins turned off the petrol to that engine, put the machine into a shallow climb and ordered everyone out. The gunner never heard the order. LAC Kenneth Gordon Reed, aged nineteen, had been shot dead in his turret.

Sgt Watkins was trapped. The cockpit escape hatch was

stuck. As he wrestled with it, the Blenheim went into a half roll and exploded, and he found himself out there, skydiving, with no more injury than a bloody nose caused by his helmet being ripped off. Ripcord pulled, parachute opened, Watkins saw James Grierson's machine with a wing on fire, and what was left of his own hurtling past him. He landed among the wreckage, between the hamlet of Merval and the small village of Lappion, north-east of Sissonne, about 15 miles from Laon. He saw Ken Reed's body. There was nothing he could do; the people of Merval would later bury him in their churchyard. He couldn't see his observer, David 'Algy' Lees. The villagers of Lappion would find the body and do the honours. The skipper, lone survivor, set off through the woods and fields.

As Watkins's machine exploded, Sgt Morrison was in section formation with Flight Lieutenant Watson and Sergeant Grierson. They managed another half-dozen miles or so. Morrison: 'On this attack a petrol feed pipe in my starboard motor was severed and the engine lost revs immediately. This threw me out of formation and as I went I saw Sgt Grierson's aircraft burst into flames.'

UX/O, captain James Grierson, fell to earth near Festieux, a village of around 500 people on the Reims road, roughly 6 miles south-east of Laon. His body and those of his two crew, Joseph Paul aged twenty-one and John Patterson aged twenty, were recovered from the wreckage by the locals and buried in their *cimetière communal*.

While Morrison wheeled away to port on his one engine to the north-east, the fighters turned their attention to the last man in the section, erstwhile leader but now with nobody to lead, George Watson in UX/M. It was no contest. Within a moment Watson, Frank Wootten and Alf Sims were hurtling down to oblivion. They fell little more than 5 miles from Grierson and 5 miles south of Laon, by the tiny village of Presles-et-Thierny, to be buried in the local churchyard. To be married, like Watson and Sims, was much more common this early in the war than it was later on, when the regulars were replaced by young volunteers who mostly thought their flying careers too uncertain for such a commitment.

In the same few seconds, as that group of Messerschmitts was destroying Watson's section, another was finishing off Delap and Co, already damaged and with their gunner incapacitated. Robert Francis Wyness had only just managed to don his parachute: 'In a matter of seconds our machine was ablaze and my pilot opened the top hatch and signalled me to bale out, which I promptly did. On the parachute opening I saw others very near the ground and saw them land, but could not see who they were before I landed myself. On my way, a fighter approached from behind and fired a few rounds at me, which missed.'

Possibly, the chutes he saw belonged to Sergeants Wrightson and Beaumont, and AC1 Thomas, the only whole crew to survive being shot down. Certainly, the chutes did not belong to Wyness's colleagues. Delap was behind him, burned by the flames but managing to launch himself clear; Pilot Officer Frank Jackson was dead. The aircraft went in at Pancy-Courtecon, another 6 miles south of Presles-et-Thierny.

F/O Fordham was in UX/B. As they took more than enough fighter fire to destroy them entirely, Fordham managed to get out and parachute to a safe landing but, looking around in what he assumed to be Belgium, or France maybe, as yet unoccupied, he couldn't find anything of his regular observer, Frank Fearnley, nor of twenty-year-old Allen Glyndwr Richards DFM, U-boat sinker; two more names for the Runnymede Memorial.

So, that was all of them, one to the flak, ten to the fighters, and Jock Morrison. 'None of my crew were hit,' he reported later, 'and it was impossible to regain formation.' Indeed it was, Sgt Morrison. There was no formation to regain.

'I dived steeply, taking evasive action. On the way down I turned the petrol to the starboard motor from outer to inner tank and the motor caught almost immediately. On levelling out at 600/700 feet, there was an explosion underneath us.'

It was a 'friendly' explosion. Messerschmitt bullets had damaged the bomb racks of UX/W and, in spite of all the switches being off, the 250lb bombs had disengaged and blown up some trees.

Morrison and observer Sgt Carbutt conferred, saw much forested countryside and a major river, which must have been the Meuse, and decided they were over the woods near Givet, to the south-west of that historic town just over the border into France. If the bigger bombs could explode on their own, so could the smaller ones, so, 'picking another heavily wooded area, I dropped the 40-pounders too so that we could force-land with some measure of safety if we had to.'

They had the track home, briefed from the target, that crossroads beyond Gembloux they had almost reached not half an hour before: off they went. Morrison: 'We were very far out in our calculations and we took a very long time to cross the Channel. I asked LAC Cleary to "home" on Watton, which he did, getting his first bearing very quickly and continuing to supply them regularly. This bearing brought us over our base.'

Delap turned his men south as the fighters appeared but Gofton, Newbatt, Toft and Christensen all went down near the target. Six more succumbed to the fighters around Laon, while Sgt Morrison turned north-east towards Givet, then west towards Amiens, on to landfall on the Sussex coast, and north-east to Watton.

They landed at 08.20. They hadn't done all that badly coming home – an hour and fifteen out to the flak at Nivelles, twenty minutes being attacked by Messerschmitts, two hours back to Watton including looking for a place to drop the 40-pounders.

'As we landed, the starboard motor petered out, due to lack of petrol, we having lost a goodly amount of petrol through the various leaks in the system, and having had trouble with airlocks in the system on the way back.'

Fifteen Messerschmitts would indeed cause 'various leaks'. 'The aircraft had to be written off, principally because the main spar in the centre section had some bullet holes in it.'

Wing Commander Bandon was there to watch his squadron return. They were late, no doubt about that: should have been back around 07.30 and it was getting on for 08.30 by the time UX/W stuttered to a halt. Taxying to the hangers on one engine in a wreck of an aeroplane was not really an option, and Paddy Bandon went up to meet the three

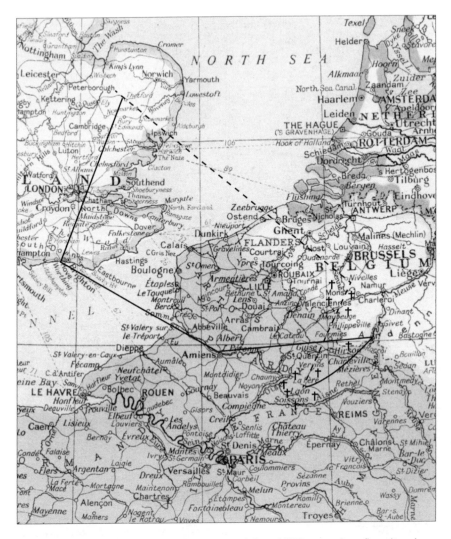

Approximate routes on 17 May and positions of downfall. The squadron flew directly to Gembloux, near Nivelles, from Watton, where the first five were hit. McConnell appeared to go down almost immediately, the only clear victory for the flak gunners, but managed another forty miles or so before having to jump near the French border, by Hirson.

shattered ghosts of aircrew who climbed out and tried to look presentable for the boss.

'Where's everybody else, Morrison?' asked the Wing Commander.

71

CHAPTER FIVE

RISING FROM THE ASHES

As the Air Ministry put it, heavy losses must be suffered in attacking vital objectives. Bomber Command losses over the whole war were about one aircraft in twenty per operation. During the Blitzkrieg that was more like one in two, but twelve out of twelve was unique even in this dangerous trade.

Morrison knew that at least four, more likely five Blenheims were not coming home. He told Bandon. Everybody saw McConnell go down. Cleary saw 'three or four', and Morrison himself had seen Grierson. That left six. They waited. The point soon came when they knew that petrol would have run out and the machines were either lost or landed elsewhere.

The first notice they would have of that was some hours away, a telephone call saying that Delap was in hospital, injured but not badly. For the moment, there were no calls from airfields. 'Everybody else' was lost, missing, but not necessarily dead. Sgt Fulbrook had been in the first machine to go down, and his adventures were very far from over:

'I left my parachute, harness etc and headed westerly, circling around behind the troops who had fired at me, and confirmed that they were French. On hearing the noise of motor transport I headed towards the nearest road and saw several light tanks and lorries with roundels painted on the front, so I came out of hiding and stopped one of them that had a parachute in the back.'

The chute belonged to WOp/AG Humphreys, who was being looked after in a nearby village. With wounds from the flak and damage from his jump, he needed more serious treatment than the locals could supply. Fulbrook was taken to see him.

'I found him with his arm and leg broken, and had his wounds dressed as far as was possible. I saw that he had an injection [morphine] before being taken to [an army] hospital at Massigny [Wassigny].'

Wassigny, a small town between Le Cateau and St Quentin, 40 miles west of Couvin where Fulbrook had landed, would soon be overrun by the advancing Germans and Humphreys would be taken prisoner. Fulbrook: 'I returned to the woods on a motor cycle and searched for F/O McConnell until 08.30.'

There was no sign of his skipper so Fulbrook gave up and began to look to himself. A French officer he met spoke good English and was happy to take him in a car to 'La Chappelle' (La Chapelle-en-Thierache) and on to St Quentin, being strafed by three Me110s on the way.

'On our arrival at St Quentin at 13.30 hours no [onward] transport was available so we went in the car to Péronne, as a train was leaving there for Paris at 15.00 hours. At about 3 miles east of this town, at a crossroads, there was a traffic jam and a Hun aircraft dropped about 70 [anti-personnel] bombs, and immediately the bombing ceased, the road was shelled for about 30 minutes.'

Fulbrook had left the car and taken what shelter he could, which was fortunate as the car was blown up in the shelling.

'The French officer and his staff had vanished, so I started to walk back to St Quentin [20 miles]. After three hours I was picked up by a motor-bus which dropped me in the square.'

This was proving to be an exciting day for Fulbrook, and it wasn't finished yet.

'I tried to find an officer but could not find one to take any interest at all, and a section of the French troops treated me as a spy and wanted to shoot me on the spot. An English-speaking Frenchman came to my rescue and I stayed with him, helping him to build a barricade on a bridge over the river Somme. We left St Quentin at approximately 19.30 hours, going to Amiens via Péronne. I reported to Amiens aerodrome at about 23.00 hours and asked for a signal to be sent to base, advising of my return.'

Time for bed, Sergeant Fulbrook. Frank Wyness, meantime, was also collecting stories for his grandchildren. He landed in a wood near Pancy-Courtecon, luckily in a clearing, if a boggy one. He stuck his parachute in a tree as a marker, thinking he might want to find his way back there, and set off to look for the parachutists he had seen land beneath him. He walked for an hour and a half before realising that the enemy had advanced rather further than he'd been led to believe.

'I saw between fifteen and twenty Hun troops, apparently searching for something or someone, possibly me. I jumped into a stream and followed it, north-westerly, keeping under cover of the banks and some overhanging trees. After running for some time I came across a column of retreating Frenchmen, who had seen my parachute and were also searching for me. They were retreating fast so I joined them, and eventually reached Braye-en-Laonnois.'

Wyness was back where he began, a mile or two from his landing ground. He picked up his parachute: 'We retired to some woods south-east of Soissons but could not reach the town as it was being bombarded. The French left me in the charge of a nurse, Mme Sorlin, who was with some Belgian refugees. From there the refugee column moved to Villers-Cotterêts.'

This was a 12-mile walk, south-west along the road that is now the N2. Villers-Cotterêts was the site of a fierce battle at the beginning of the First World War, during the retreat from Mons. The Germans would not meet such resistance this time but they weren't there yet and the column turned north-west towards Compiègne.

'We were bombarded by Hun aircraft. After lying under cover for three hours, we carried on along the railway line to a point where trains were running and finally reached Paris at 06.00, 19th of May.'

After 60 miles on foot, carrying his parachute, he reported to the British Air Attaché in Paris who sent him to the

Medical Officer for a check-up. That was fine, so he boarded a Lockheed Electra (as flown by Amelia Earhart when she disappeared, a similar aircraft to the DC2 Dakota) at Le Bourget, arrived at Hendon 15.15, got a train to Brandon in Norfolk, arriving 22.05. It is not recorded if he still had his chute with him when he turned up at RAF Watton.

The 17th was an eventful day on both sides of the Channel for the Watkins family. About an hour after the sergeant was shot down, Mrs Watkins gave birth to a daughter, and a couple of hours later the telegram came telling her that her husband was missing. He was, but not permanently.

He was walking south-west, hiding as he went from German soldiers who seemed to be everywhere. When he heard two men conversing behind a haystack, he drew his service revolver, the standard .38 Enfield No. 2, and confronted them. Two privates of the French army immediately surrendered to the superior power of the RAF and the three of them set off walking together. Some three hours later they reached a village, by which time Watkins's injured knee was swollen to an enormous size and the shrapnel in his shoulder was painful. An ambulance was found and he was put in it, bound for Reims, where he spotted an RAF officer who turned out to be F/O Fordham, B Flight, 82 Squadron. Forgetting his swollen knee, Watkins jumped from the ambulance and, with Fordham, decided on a plan.

They made their way south to Épernay, thence to Cherbourg, where they were evacuated with remnants of 105 Squadron, a Fairey Battle unit of the AASF which had virtually ceased to exist after heavy losses in the first week of Blitzkrieg. Watkins and Fordham were back at Watton a fortnight after they were shot down.

Les Wrightson and Stan Beaumont, with AC1 Thomas, had not had an easy time of it either. The pilot, Wrightson, had been badly hurt in his parachute landing and the other two had to carry him. They joined a flood of refugees, caught a train to Paris and journeyed on many miles to Nantes, on the Biscay coast, where the captain of a French fishing boat agreed to take them back to England.

Back at Watton on that dreadful morning, Jock Morrison and his crew went through the debrief – called the interrogation – with the intelligence officer, doubtless grateful for the tea and free cigarettes. Out on the airfield, in the messes, in the flight offices, in the control tower, there was a stunned silence for two hours. Ground crew, working as it were on autopilot, confirmed the status of Morrison's machine as a write-off. People wandered about, or sat in confusion, wondering how such a thing could be. Paddy Bandon began making plans to reform his squadron.

At 10.30, F/O Charlie Breese arrived from his fighter escort duties in France and Bandon told him the news. The establishment on 10 May had been twenty-two Blenheims. Now, assuming the other three got back from France, there were ten. Bandon knew very well that this sort of damage could result – at the least – in a short-term amalgamation with another squadron; but headquarters had decided on something more drastic. Before midday, the phone call came saying that No. 82 Squadron was to be shared out among the other hard-pressed squadrons and would therefore be no more.

Bandon's response was very firm indeed. Eleven crews were missing with no word so far of survivors and, assuming that Morrison's first-hand knowledge was applied to the rest of the operation, there might well not be any. Those men could not be dishonoured in this abrupt manner. Their squadron must live on, and Paddy Bandon would see that it did.

The wing commander got his way and began making inquiries, to be interrupted at 16.30 by the other three escorts landing back home. Captains Sutcliffe, Hunt and Atkinson were called in and given the story. There was still no news of anyone, but hope must not be given up. In any case, most of A Flight was still alive and well, and Bandon had every intention of getting the squadron up to strength within days, so the boys had better be ready to operate again soon.

Next day was Saturday the 18th. Messages came in to say that F/O Fordham and Sgts Fulbrook and Watkins were safe, so their families could be told to ignore yesterday's telegrams, and Fulbrook could tell Bandon about Humphreys, in hospital. Four officer pilots arrived from elsewhere to begin the rebuilding programme (other ranks' arrivals were not noted in the ORB) and Paddy Bandon led them up on a practice flight.

A copy of Friday's *London Gazette* arrived at the station on Sunday. It announced the DFC for Sq/Ldr Walter Philip Sutcliffe, for his photography under intense AA fire on 20 March, surveying the seaplane base at Hornum (Sylt). Sergeant Reg Newbatt, late of Gembloux, only had MID for the same op, while their crews, including Algy Lees and Ken Reed who were killed at Gembloux in Watkins's aircraft, got nothing.

OPERATIONS RECORD BOOK.

R.A.F. Form 541.

Appendix

DETAIL OF WORK CARRIED OUT.

By .... 82 SQUADRON

No. of pages used for day.

Aircraft Type and No.	Crew.	Duty.	Time Up.	Time Down.	Details of Sortie or Flight	Reference.
Blenheim Mk IV P4852 O P4839 T	S/Ldr Delap. Sgt Wyness P/O Jackson. P/O McConnell Sgt Fulbrook A/O Humphreys	Raid SHERLOUK Ops 9	0450	0650	The 12 aircraft took off the raid SHERLOUK. Heavy A.A. fire was encountered before reaching the objective and the Squadron opened up formation and took evasive action. P/O McConnell was seen to go down. The formation was then attacked by 15 Me.109s before they were able to reform close formation. Sgt Morrison and his crew were the only crew who returned. None of this crew was injured, although the aircraft was very badly damaged by A.A.fire and E.A.fire (both cannon and machine gun). This crew reported that they were flying at 2000000 ft when attacked. They saw Sgt Grierson's aircraft hit and go down in flames and also two other Blenheims, which they were unable to identify, going down in flames.	
P4903 V	Sgt Wrightson Sgt Beaumont A/O Thomas					
P4838 R	P/O Gurton Sgt Miller Cpl Cummins					
P4862 Y	P/O Christenson Sgt Phillips LAC Ettershank					
P4854 F	P/O Turk Sgt Grouch A/O Norris					
P4815 M	P/Lt Watson Sgt Wootton A/O Sims					

The bleak story of May 17, entered in the records as far as current information allowed, was signed off at the end of the month by Squadron Leader 'Rusty' Wardell, himself fated to appear in a similarly sparse report later in the summer.

Another officer pilot arrived that afternoon, and that evening a young WOp/AG sat down to write a letter home. He was Fred Thripp, age nineteen, in the RAF since April

Aircraft Type and No.	Crew	Duty.	Time Up.	Time Down.	Details of Sortie or Flight.	References.
Blenheim Mk IV P9210 O	Sgt Grierson Sgt Paul AO Patterson					
P9266 W	Sgt Morrison Sgt Garbutt AO Cleary					
N6651 F	P/O Fordham Sgt Fearnley Cpl Richards					
P4925 D	Sgt Newbatt Sgt Greasley Sgt Knowles					
N6604 B	Sgt Watkins Sgt Ross AO Reed					

1938, with 82 Squadron since January 1939. He'd been on the fighter escort trip with F/Lt Joe Hunt:

Dear Mum Dad Rene & Harry.
Well here we are again, but not in quite the same spirit. I suppose that you heard about those eleven

machines failing to return from the raid on Brussels, well they were all ours. Nine were from B flight and 2 were from A flight. Some of them escaped and are in hospital, and there is quite possibly some more hanging around that we have not heard of yet. My best pal was in one of them and we know definitely that he was killed. ['Best pal' was LAC Ken Reed, the only WOp/AG so far to be confirmed dead.]

It was only by a miracle that they [Morrison and crew] got back, as the engines cut as they landed through loss of oil and petrol. The A.G. had the narrowest escape anyone has ever had. His turret was shot to pieces, his gun hit, holes all over the fuselage. The armour plating did its work very successfully.

It was only by chance that all A flight were not on it, but the rest of us were over in France having a good time. We had to navigate some fighters over to different dromes, then by a prearranged plan we all met on one drome. You should have seen the stuff we brought back with us. And of course we all sold the stuff at a profit to us and the chaps themselves. They can get 50 cigarettes for 1s/6d so we brought quite a number back beside some liquid. [As opposed to 30, generally at 6d for a packet of ten. One shilling and sixpence would be about £3.50 today.]

We had an air raid soon after we landed [in France], but nobody takes any notice of them, you just carry on, listening to the guns and watching the smoke puffs in the air. We landed on one drome which had been bombed only a couple of nights before. I can nearly find my way over France now by just looking at the towns. It was very pitiful to see the refugees going along the roads, with a couple of blankets and a few odds and ends strapped onto their cycles, with no place to go, yet all going in the same direction. We could just make out what they were trying to say to us, about good luck and all of the rest of it. But it was quite an education, all through the whole trip. I always looked on the old war stories with a certain amount of doubt but it is just as they say. The cookhouses are small tents hidden in the trees.

Well I could tell you a lot more but that can wait for a while, until leave periods start coming round again. We are waiting for some new machines to come in now. Then we get going again with what is left of us. Cheerio for now.

With Love.

Fred

PS If you will I should like some more of that sulphur ointment for my face, and perhaps some Yeast-Vites. I hear now that we go into the attack tomorrow with our remaining six.

It would seem that Fred, like many teenage boys, suffered from acne, to be treated the traditional way with sulphur.

Mum, Dad, Rene and Harry may well have heard about the eleven missing aircraft. The Air Ministry had released a statement on the evening of the 17th, which was reported in all the papers the next day. *The Times* carried the story, beneath headlines that read 'RAF Still Attacking, Bombs on Enemy Supplies, Heavy German Losses' and beneath a deal of copy about fierce and determined attacks inflicting great damage. One paragraph said: 'In support of the French Army, a squadron of Blenheims made a sortie this morning to bomb a key position at Gembloux. They encountered a large formation of enemy fighters and intense AA fire. In spite of great gallantry and determination 11 of our aircraft failed to return.'

Air Ministry statements were a curious mixture of propaganda, gloss, and the stark truth. On the same page of *The Times* was a piece headed 'Losses Compared', suggesting that the Germans had lost over 1,000 aircraft since the start of the Blitzkrieg, not to forget the losses sustained in Poland and Norway.

> Today's German High Command *communiqué* gave the losses of Allied aircraft as 1,462. It is thought that the High Command must have published their own loss in error. Allied losses are in fact only a small fraction of the German machines.
>
> In spite of these heavy inroads into the fighting strength of the German Air Force it must be understood that their reserves are considerable, and that they are for a time, at least, able to sustain their effort.

The Times Aeronautical Correspondent further commented: 'It is accepted that during the whole of the past week's intensive aerial warfare in France and Belgium the technical superiority of British aircraft over those of the enemy has been demonstrated even more convincingly than during the earlier minor engagements.'

Fred Thripp, who must have known rather more about fractional losses and technical superiority than *Times* journalists, had written that he expected to be on the attack again the next day, the 20th, and so he was. Orders had gone out that, in view of the disastrous results so far, 2 Group and the remnants of the AASF and the Air Component were to fly only at night. It was never explained quite how 1940 bomber crews were expected to find small moving targets, such as groups of armoured vehicles, in the dark, with no more navigation aids than a walker on the fells. Then, having found said target, ill met by moonlight perhaps, they were supposed to destroy it while being unable to see it properly.

During the day of Monday 20 May, the eight Blenheims remaining of Air Component squadron No. 18, landed at Watton from France. At 21.35 and 22.05, two sections of three Blenheims of 82 Squadron took off for the road between Geraardsbergen (Grammont) and Oudenaarde (Audenarde), about 30 miles west of Brussels, where there was an armoured column. In the lead was Paddy Bandon, with WOp/AG Leading Aircraftman Thripp, both of them no doubt thinking about those eleven machines and crews failing to return but never for a moment questioning their duty as a fact of wartime life. With them were four new pilots and old boy P/O Atkinson, with a mixture of new and old hands as crew.

If the expectation was that two separate sections of three

crews might each fly to and find a particular panzer unit on a particular road at night, then somebody wasn't thinking straight. A more realistic task would have been to fly to the area and attack targets of opportunity, which was what happened.

One of the six came back early with mechanical trouble. On a misty night, two crews found a target that they believed was on the Halle–Leerbeek road, 12 miles south-west of Brussels and bombed from 2,000 feet. Another crew dropped their bombs near the little town of Galmaarden (Gammerages), around 6 miles east of Geraardsbergen, all at once (in salvo) as their Mickey Mouse was u/s (unserviceable). The control used by the observer to select which bombs to drop was a small panel of switches with a clockwork mechanism, all of which, looked perhaps, very vaguely, like a Mickey Mouse watch, or perhaps this was an early instance of that term being applied to something not really up to its job.

The other two came home with their loads intact, having been unable to find anything to bomb, and the overall effect was negligible. Night raids of this sort were worse than useless. Aircrews were still in danger – 'All forms of AA fire were encountered and searchlights were numerous and effective' – although there was no threat from fighters. More important from Ugly Barratt's point of view, night bombing was doing nothing at all to hinder the Germans. He asked for daylights to be brought back.

The policy at 2 Group was that daylights could only be mounted with fighter escort or cloud cover, neither of which could be reliably arranged, and even if they were so mounted, the results were hardly encouraging. Just a few hours between target assignment and attack often meant the target was no longer there but rather those few hours further into the enemy's short-term objective: to encircle and trap the British Expeditionary Force.

Fred Thripp was up and away again next day as WOp/AG with the CO, and with the Germans well into the Pas-de-Calais, heading rapidly towards completing the circle. Trying to stop them as they roared along the road from Hesdin towards Boulogne were three of No. 82 in a joint op with nine of 21 Squadron, scheduled to meet another dozen from 107, for whom it was the second raid of the day. Near Montreuil, only 6 miles from the fishing port of Étaples and the elegant holiday resort of Le Touquet, bombs were seen to hit and near-miss, and as they returned so six more of 82 plus three of 18 Squadron, lately based in France, headed for the same region led by Walter Sutcliffe.

They would have fighter escorts, Spitfires, so there should be no trouble from Messerschmitts. As if to prove that you were never safe in a bomber in daylight, when the formation was almost at the appointed rendezvous with the escorts, six Spitfires flew across their line and fell in behind. This was odd, because escorts normally flew above, 1,000 feet or so, ready to dive down on any peregrines attacking their pigeons.

Just how odd became clear immediately, as one of the Spitfire pilots, the leader, went for the 18 Squadron Blenheim skippered by P/O Viv Rees and shot large pieces off the port engine. He also managed to hit fuel tanks and port aileron but missed everything on the starboard side and most of what was in the middle, including all the crew. Bomber crews expected this sort of thing when flying over His Majesty's warships, the sailor boys being notoriously poor at aircraft recognition, but it was something of a shock coming from their own RAF.

Rees thought he could get down, which was better than jumping, and so headed for Boulogne. Once over that town and 5 miles on, he found a decent landing space near the small seaside resort of Wimereux. Coming in, he realised that the Spit had rendered his landing gear u/s and so had to belly flop. This was still a German-free area, and the crew could get themselves back to Boulogne and on to Watton next day. What happened to the Spitfire pilot is not recorded.

Keeping a careful eye out for friends and enemies, the rest pressed on to find 'columns of tanks and lorries at 20 yard spacing north of Le Touquet'. They went in low, down to 1,500 feet, dropped their bombs, and came around again to strafe the enemy on the road. Bombs hit, fires were started, there were explosions, but a few gallant Blenheim crews could only do so much.

The situation was indeed desperate. The Germans had reached the Channel coast at Abbeville on the 20th and had turned north, with a large swath of Belgium and France behind them, bordered more or less by the river Somme. Le Touquet marked a point 45 miles or so south of Dunkirk. They were also on the North Sea coast in The Netherlands, which had surrendered on the 15th, and, despite last-gasp resistance in Zeeland, the enemy effectively controlled the whole country and its aerodromes. In the middle was the British Expeditionary Force, what was left of the Belgian army and large components of French.

The BEF was cornered and launched a counter-offensive from Arras towards the Bapaume–Péronne gap, where there was a perceived opportunity to break through the German corridor along the Somme valley – that is, the space of some 30 miles between the isolated Allies and 'mainland' France. The French changed their supreme commander, causing delays, and though they came at the same objective from the south, they were compelled to fall back. The gap had shrunk to not much more than 10 miles but there was no breakthrough. The BEF was doomed, and all that 2 Group had left to help were 60 serviceable Blenheims.

Eighteen of them went back to Hesdin, 22 May, a joint op for 82 and 21 Squadrons. They found some tanks and transport standing in the road at Hubersent, a few miles north-west of Le Touquet. They dive-bombed the targets in sections of three, line astern, and almost got away with it. There were direct hits on the vehicles but there was also one on a Blenheim of 82, its observer one of the old boys, Sergeant Fred Phillipson, age 27, married to Elsie. He'd flown with Sutcliffe on the French fighter escort jaunt, so missing the mayhem of 17 May but not missing the same fate for long. The skipper, Sergeant John Hartfield, and the WOp/AG AC2 Angus Elliot were killed, too, so that was the end of their 82 Squadron experience: four days.

Also on this day, Squadron Leader George Hall of 110 Squadron, late of No. 82 - he of the falling-over drink trick - and his crew were killed, shot down by the Abbeville flak.

During the night of 22/23 May, the Germans launched a surprise attack on the fort at La Crèche, near Wimereux, originally a Napoleonic defence against the British but now modernised with formidable guns and a significant obstacle for the Germans as they gathered around Boulogne. For the Allies, Boulogne wasn't just another city to fight for; it was the main evacuation port, where the wounded could be sent home.

The Germans' night attack failed as the garrison spun their cannons round to fire inland, but another attempt in daylight succeeded. The naval response was to send a small flotilla of Royal Navy and French warships to shell the fort, to try to destroy the guns.

One aerial response was to send three Blenheims of 82 Squadron in the evening, led by F/Lt Hunt with Fred Thripp in the turret. By this time, the Germans were in possession and the flotilla was bombarding. ORB: 'The first run was ruined by several Allied destroyers which fired continuously at our aircraft in spite of correct recognition procedure.' Even so, the Blenheims went around again and bombed some German tanks. Crews noted that the fort was damaged, so the navy was getting something right.

The news was worse the next day, Friday 24 May, two weeks into the German invasion. Boulogne had fallen. The BEF had nowhere to go except home, via Calais and Dunkirk, and the Germans were not going to allow that. Boulogne to Calais is hardly 20 miles as the crow flies or, indeed, as the tanks raced along the main road that is now the A16/E402. About two-thirds of the way is the village of St Inglevert, and the panzers were rattling through there on that same morning. Six of 82 Squadron took off with six of 21, fighter escorts were met, and by midday they were bombing the enemy north-east of

St Inglevert, towards Calais, and blowing holes in the road if no tank hits could be claimed.

British reinforcements had arrived in Calais in a great rush, with orders to push out. Attempts to do this proved very expensive, while the Germans, obviously planning to attend to Calais when they had a moment, skirted round the place and headed for Dunkirk.

That evening, Paddy Bandon, with his favourite WOp/AG Fred Thripp in the turret, led six to a spot about halfway between those two ports, near Gravelines. Again, it was holes in the road but no tanks hit.

Headquarters at 2 Group issued an order of the day that surely cannot have been gratefully received by aircrew flying out to face the flak and the fighters every morning and afternoon: 'It must be impressed upon leaders that risks must be taken in this emergency to find the really important targets, and attack them.'

Really? And what else?

'It must now be accepted that the day has passed when attacks can be launched at definite targets as a result of previous reconnaissance. This is due to the rapidity of movement of enemy forces.'

You don't say. So that's what's been happening.

The statement closed with another stab at the obvious: 'In view of the critical situation of the BEF it is essential that all attacks are pressed home with vigour.'

The Germans were coming from the east as well as the south. Some 2 Group squadrons kept on bombing in the Calais region, while 82 went for that stretch of the river Lys between Menen (Menin) and Kortrijk (Courtrai) the Germans were trying to cross. Bridges were the targets, old ones and the pontoons the enemy had built, and most attacks were made by single aircraft, dive-bombing through heavy concentrations of AA fire or, like the man said, taking risks to press attacks home with vigour. Six went at dawn, and six more in the afternoon and, surprisingly, they all came home again.

On 26 May 1940, it was decided by the War Cabinet to evacuate the BEF by sea, along with any of the French and Belgian forces that could be saved. The order for Operation Dynamo was given at 18.57 hours.

A couple of pontoon bridges destroyed may have delayed the German advance but next day it had reached St Omer, 20 miles from Dunkirk, and that's where 82 and 21 Squadrons were sent, mid-afternoon on 27 May. German lorries and tanks were assembled in considerable numbers on the eastern side of St Omer, near Arques and Blendeques, and there was a likely looking warehouse, so they picked their targets and hit them. Whether the targets were really important the leaders could not have said, but the risks were clear enough, from the flak and from a flight of Me110s. When AC1 Crozier, with P/O McKenzie, saw one firing at another of his section, he banged away with no fewer than 1,000 rounds at it. 'The Me110 half rolled and fell away into the cloud, and did not renew the encounter.'

On the way back, crews saw Stukas dive-bombing Calais. It was by air power that the Germans expected to produce the surrender of that town, now under siege, and destroy the BEF in their last stronghold, Dunkirk.

It was St Omer again next day at dawn, as the great embarkation began, with the BEF falling back towards the port from its defensive line. The Germans were coming from every direction, from above – although the weather and the RAF prevented them from ever claiming complete air superiority at Dunkirk – from Boulogne to the west, Ostend and Antwerp to the east, Lille to the south. The flyers of 82 picked up their fighter escort at Northolt and, crossing what was now the enemy coast, encountered enough flak to split them all up, bombers and fighters. Still, nobody went down so they could press on to attack more of the never-ending stream of armour, while Joe Hunt, now a squadron leader, could delight Fred Thripp and the long-suffering observer Sgt Bish Bareham, with a spectacularly successful, 'thorough and accurate' reconnaissance of the German lines from Watten to Aire.

King Leopold of the Belgians announced their capitulation on that day, 28 May, which removed a large part of the BEF's support to the north. As the evacuation continued, the Luftwaffe cursed the bad weather that hindered their bombing of Dunkirk, while 82 Squadron called it 'excellent cloud cover' for a raid deep into Belgium, on a road headed for the coast through Diksmuide and neighbouring village Esen. Frank Wyness and Walter Sutcliffe had had their medals pinned on them by King George three days before. Now Sutcliffe went in very low, wrecked a few vehicles and knocked a house down that blocked the road. They saw a single Me110 but it stood off.

All that mattered now was to keep the enemy at bay long enough for the BEF to get on their armada of ships and boats, large and small. There was no longer any thought of beating the Germans back, but at least 2 Group could deploy every resource to holding them up. That the resource was only three-score light bombers didn't come into it. Losses hadn't been so bad lately, only nine since the 25th.

There were no losses today, either, the 30th, although there was flak damage as the cloud forced the bombers down to 400 feet so they could see what they were hitting, which was more tanks and transport between Veurne (Furnes) and Diksmuide. Nine crews attacked seven different targets, while five other squadrons put in fifty-eight sorties between them, so that was just about everything 2 Group could offer.

The *Luftwaffemeister* Göring had not delivered an air-imposed Dunkirk submission as promised but the Wehrmacht was massing for a major offensive against the town. So far, some superbly brave fighting by French units had delayed the Germans, as of course had the RAF, but the enemy was attacking hard. They came up against defensive forces along the 1914 Belgian–German front line, from Nieuwpoort on the coast, inland through the village of Pervijze, which had been destroyed in the Great War, to Diksmuide, and tried to drive in from the east between Diksmuide and Poperinge.

At dawn on 31 May, the first raids for 82 Squadron were on that latter area, close to Vleteren, where the Trappist beer comes from. They also hit the Pervijze–Diksmuide road and other targets, the eight Blenheims led by Paddy Bandon bombing wherever there was a possibility of useful wrecking. The squadron, desperately stretched, also sent nine in the afternoon to bridges at Nieuwpoort. Two of the crews had already been on the morning raid; one pilot went again with a different crew, and one WOp/AG went again with a different pilot; three of the squadron's aircraft did both trips. Bish Bareham and Fred Thripp, after breakfast with Bandon, spent teatime with Joe Hunt. They missed the bridges but blocked the roads leading thereto, and these efforts on Nieuwpoort, followed up by other 2 Group squadrons, actually succeeded in bringing the Germans to a temporary halt.

It is impossible to overstate the courage of these men, flying into a curtain of hot metal in the morning, somehow surviving, then filling up with petrol and bombs and doing the whole thing again in the afternoon. Each time they went, it was in the knowledge that other young men, some of them known personally, had been doing just the same thing when they were killed yesterday.

Meanwhile, the stiff social strata of RAF ranks were being shaken slightly. An Air Ministry directive was issued on 1 June 1940 that all aircrew below the rank of sergeant were to be promoted to that rank, which meant a pay rise of an extra shilling and sixpence a day or even more. This was all much to the shocked disgust of long-serving RAF regular sergeants who had taken ten or fifteen years to get those tapes on their arms. Now every Tom, Dick and Harry, no matter how wet behind the ears, was a sergeant if he was aircrew. The sergeants' mess, depending on who was in, could often become a mess of two parts. Never mind officers and other ranks; sergeants and erks had never mixed much before. So, Fred Thripp was a sergeant.

The great evacuation of Dunkirk was passing its peak and

there was a change in the objectives of operations. There was a recco of Terneuzen area – nothing much to report – and no ops on 2 June, then a major one on the 3rd, bombing shore installations of guns aimed at the last of the rescue fleet. With fighter cover, the Blenheims took it in turns to fly low over the batteries, keeping them quiet with bombs and bullets.

The Germans could have made their own embarkation, with greatly superior numbers in army and in air force to cover, and invaded Britain. The French were not going to strike back. Instead, Hitler chose to complete his demolition of France and leave the British for later.

Whatever the timescale, there was no doubting the new threat posed by the Luftwaffe on its many new and advanced air bases, and the British war bosses thought it would be good if some of that threat could be forced back into Germany, on the defensive. The night bombers were already flying to German targets. Could the day bombers, the Blenheims of 2 Group, add to the effect? Yes, but only on cloudy days.

Watton station was given a list of oil refineries at Hanover, Bremen and so on, and a start date: 5 June. The other stations had their own lists, and missions were to be flown every third day, in between continuing with the work they had been doing, attacking armoured columns as they drove further into France. The oil-in-Germany attacks were to be sporadic and widely spaced. The Germans were to suffer the pain of a thousand small cuts.

Despite the order for promotion, on 3 June Messrs Thripp, Crozier, Clarke and Co were still listed as aircraftmen; but on the 8th it was Sergeant John Byatt who was brought home dead in P/O Percival's machine after they'd been found by a flock of Me109s while blowing up a petrol dump at Abbeville. That aircraft never flew again, and neither did Sergeant Brian Burt, the only crew member killed when P/O Robertson's Blenheim was also the victim of fighters on the same op, and it was Sergeant Clarke, flying with P/O Keeble, who had the rare achievement of shooting down a Messerschmitt from a Blenheim.

Earlier in the day, it had been Sergeant Crozier taken prisoner with P/O McKenzie when they were shot down on another raid against AFVs near Noyon, and on the 9th it was Sergeant Thripp who was wounded by flak, on a similar op against transport and infantry.

Fred was posted to an OTU (Operational Training Unit) as an instructor. He would come back to 82 Squadron in February 1941, fly his fiftieth op in the April, then move to Malta with 110 Squadron. After scoring direct hits on a power station at Tripoli, his Blenheim would be shot down by an Italian fighter, a Fiat CR42, and crash into the sea.

Frederick Samuel Thripp, of Totternhoe, Bedfordshire, still only twenty years old, a lad who had been on so many ops and narrowly avoided death so many times by Me109 cannon, was killed by machine-gun fire from a 1930s fixed-undercarriage biplane. The CR42 was exceptionally fast for a biplane, with a top speed similar to the Blenheim's, and so manoeuvrable that Spitfire and Hurricane pilots avoided getting into close-combat dogfights, but Fred's captain was a greatly experienced wing commander who must have been taken by surprise.

The German oil-refinery plan, optimistically expanded to include daylight raids on all kinds of industrial targets, was never going to be worthwhile. Certainly it didn't start on time; after early cloud, 5 June was a beautiful sunny day, one of many in that glorious summer, and the weather was too fine for flying the next day too, but by the 7th matters were deemed so desperate that the Blenheims had to go, clear skies or not. The enemy had turned his attention from Dunkirk and the BEF to Paris and the French.

For the next week or so, the squadron was in the air every day looking for panzers and transport, always attacked by flak, often attacked by fighters even when there were escorts, and ever further on to the south-west as the armour closed on the river Seine. At the RAF wireless school in Wiltshire some of the students had unexpected news. A young fellow called John Bristow was ordered to the office and told that they were short of WOp/AGs at 82 Squadron because so many had been lost at Gembloux. Bristow:

I hadn't actually finished the wireless course, although that didn't matter too much because I'd been working as a radio engineer before I joined, but I was now an air gunner and I had never seen a machine gun. That was June 9th, when I was AC1 Bristow. Next day, I was Sergeant Bristow. [The squadron was attacking near Rouen, beside the Seine, not that he knew that.]
Turning up at Watton I was taken down to the firing range and shown a Vickers K. I thought it was the worst put together bit of ironmongery I'd ever

seen, but we had to fire it and strip it down, and the following day, would you believe it, I was joe'd to use the damn thing on an op.

Bristow, like all his WOp/AG colleagues in those days, had to know a great deal about the workings and practicalities of wireless to be able to get his unreliable and temperamental kit to work in the unforgiving circumstances of hostile flight. Now he had a similarly unreliable gun in his charge that he knew almost nothing about. At least he could be comforted with the thought on this first trip that his pilot and observer, whom he was supposed to defend with said gun, had both been on ops before. Anyway, they went to Le Havre, the Seine estuary. They saw no tanks, and they were not disturbed by fighters so Sgt Bristow remained a machine-gun virgin, and they came home with their bombs.

On 12 June, as the Germans entered Paris, Bristow was up again but with a different crew just north of Le Havre, again no losses for the squadron, but that run of luck finished at Le Gault la Forêt, way over to the east of Paris in the Reims/Épernay area, where an allegedly huge concentration of tanks brought raids all day. The promised French fighter cover did not materialise and three out of nine 82 Squadron Blenheims were shot down, with two of 21 Squadron flying from Bodney, plus five France-based Battles.

Why the 82 Squadron crew captained by Sergeant Albert Merritt should fall into the Waddenzee, well north of Amsterdam, can only be guessed at. Being so far off track on a 'routine' daylight raid, even though there was rain and cloud about, must have meant damage over the target, possibly a dead or wounded observer, or a wrecked turret meaning no wireless to get a fix.

There were three categories of fix at this time. A first-class fix was obtained when three ground stations on the UK mainland bounced a radio signal off the aircraft and, receiving a strong signal back, found their intersecting point. The position was calculated, probably within a mile, and transmitted to the aircraft. Lesser degrees of confidence, due to weakness of signal or fewer ground stations receiving, produced second- and third-class fixes. As bad weather interfered with the process, poorer quality fixes had to be given when precision was most needed.

UX/X crashed near the target with only the WOp/AG, Ken Harris DFM, being killed. Charlie Breese and his observer were taken prisoner. P/O Eyton-Williams, a new pilot, kept his machine up long enough to reach more friendly territory but was injured in the crash. The observer, Sgt Carbutt, was anything but new. He'd seen all that action on 17 May with Morrison. He, the officer and his mate, WOp/AG Sgt Augustus Spencer Beeby, kept ahead of the Germans and returned to Watton. Gus Beeby was one of the new boys brought in immediately after Gembloux, so he'd only been on the squadron three weeks. He stated: 'Our skipper was wounded by the flak but he managed to crash-land about three miles beyond where the Germans were. We got him out, set fire to the aircraft, and looked for help. There was a French officer in a van that we stopped, and he arranged an ambulance for the skipper to take him away.'

The rest of the journey was a bit of a muddle. Every time Beeby and Carbutt reached a place where they thought their captain would be, he'd been moved on.

'We made our way towards the coast, travelling on trains and cattle trucks with the refugees, until we reached Bordeaux, where we got a boat home.'

It had taken them a fortnight. Eyton-Williams too reached Blighty somehow and he was put on the Active List, that is, generally restricted to non-flying duties but could be called upon in an emergency. There is no record of 82 Squadron calling upon him. The other two were soon flying on ops again – Carbutt with another returner, Sq/Ldr Delap, although he would crew up regularly with P/O Fordham, who had survived 17 May and many other scrapes and could be said to be a lucky skipper.

Beeby's first after evading would be with the new CO, Wing Commander Lart, on 7 July, a quite remarkable flight (see below). Aircrew flying with Lart found him a very exciting driver indeed, and for Beeby this would prove a fateful relationship.

Paddy Bandon's last op was an anti–climax, an early morning tank job when he had to turn his two sections back because the weather was too good without fighter escort, but after 18 June when they hit the roads to Cherbourg, there were no more tank raids for 82 Squadron. The battle for France was almost over. The French asked for armistice terms on the 17th and it was time for another battle to begin.

RAF attacks began on ex–Allied airfields; the British were getting their retaliation in first and, in effect, starting the Battle of Britain. The squadron went to Merville aerodrome, and Amiens, where they set aircraft on fire and wrecked hangars. They came back from Schiphol because there was no cloud at all and, in the middle of the newly appreciated invasion threat, resumed German industrial duties. To avoid losses, the latter type of raid could only be mounted in poor weather, which also made it more difficult to find the targets. If the weather turned fine, crews had to abort. Frequently, the result was a frustrated returning crew dropping their bombs on Schiphol or similar. ORB, 21 June:

> 10 aircraft despatched singly to attack targets in the Ruhr and at Bremen and Hanover. Sq/Ldr Hunt attacked oil refineries at Bremen. Sq/Ldr Sutcliffe approached the Ruhr but returned owing to uncertainty of balloon positions. He released his bombs on Haanslede aerodrome on the return journey. Sgt Watkins bombed Schipol [*sic*] aerodrome. Other aircraft returned owing to lack of cloud cover.

Watkins was John Bristow's pilot. Bristow:
One of the worst targets we had at that time was Schiphol, which was quite highly defended. We went there one day, just a single aircraft, and got in and dropped our bombs. We actually hit the drome but whether we hit the aircraft or the hangars we didn't quite know. A squadron of 109s came up and intercepted us. Luckily, there was a cloud bank over the airfield which we dived into very quickly and

Below: The Mark I Blenheim was a revolution that had been too long coming. It was fast for its time and met all the specifications for a tactical light/medium bomber, but insufficient thought had been given to the way crews would have to operate in war.

Above: Standard equipment for 82 Squadron in the First World War, the Armstrong Whitworth FK8 was a fairly big beast for its time. Like all British aircraft not specifically designed as fighters, it was expected to do everything else while defending itself, including bombing, reconnaissance, artillery spotting, ground-troops support, supplies dropping, tactical photography and anything more called for by the army. On a still day, loaded only with crew, it could make 95mph in level flight.

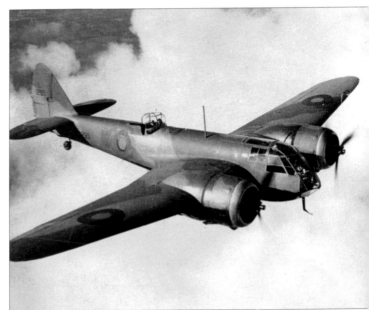

You can see why people found the Blenheim so exciting. This, the Handley Page Heyford Mark III, was still in RAF service when the Blenheim came on strength. It could not get to Germany and back with a decent load of bombs, and top speed was 142mph, much less when loaded.

Right: Paddy Delap brought back this photograph of U31 to much excitement. Nobody in the RAF had sunk a U-boat before or, indeed, any kind of warship in open sea, or on purpose. Delap had the DFC for it, and his crew each had the DFM.

Left: From the left, in front of a Blenheim: Sq/Ldr Walter Sutcliffe DFC, W/C Paddy Bandon, F/O Robert McConnell, F/O D A Fordham, F/Lt George Hall. McConnell and Fordham would be shot down on 17 May, both surviving. Hall, promoted to Squadron Leader and transferred to 110 Squadron, would be killed in action, his Blenheim shot down by flak over the Somme.

Right: The abandoned earl in peacetime authority (left), in the 1960s and at the top of the RAF, enjoys a joke as ever as he makes a return visit to RAF Watton.

F/O Lart spent the first and lengthiest part of his air force career at Kohat in India (now in Pakistan), not far from the Afghan border and the Khyber Pass. Squadron equipment was the DH9A (flying photo), then the Westland Wapiti.

Left: The squadron reborn – the replacement aircraft after Gembloux, photographed at Watton in July 1940 by 82 Squadron observer Sgt Bish Bareham. R3802 UX/A would be Ellen's machine at Ålborg, R3904 UX/K Newland's, R3821 UX/N Hale's.

Right: Me109 pilot of 5 Staffel, Jagdgeschwader 77, Gefreiter (Cpl) Heinrich Brunsmann, took part in the fight on 13 August but, according to him, did not score. This was one of his first operations and, in the excitement of closing in on a vulnerable Blenheim, he forgot to remove the safety catch.

Armourers sorting out cannon and machine-gun ammunition, ready for loading into the fighters. The two Me109 in the picture both flew in the battle of 13 August.

Left: A Danish policeman looks grimly at a German photographer as two more of the occupying troops make the necessary notes. This is the remainder of the tail section of T1993, perhaps arranged neatly for the picture having fallen some yards away from the rest of the machine.

Right: As well as the many official photographs taken at this fine PR opportunity, there was at least one amateur with an eye for a picture. Here we see R3800 UX/Z in its final dive, upside down, before hitting the fjord shore not far from the sea-plane base. The photographer would have seen two parachutists emerge, so he might well have known that inside 'his' Blenheim there was a third man.

Left: Sgts Blair, Magrath and Greenwood survived this crash. This photograph was taken by Eghold resident Henry Jensen who, like anyone looking at it, must have wondered how anyone could have lived through such a catastrophic event. He knew first-hand that they had, as he had been among the helpers who brought the three airmen ashore.

Above: F/Lt Syms, ankle broken in his parachute jump, is provided with a much needed smoke by his German guard, who looks out towards the sea-plane base.

Right: His German captors seem rather more amused at the situation than does Sgt Wright, Syms's observer.

Left: Germans dragging a body from the crater made by R3821 UX/N. There is very little left that is recognisable as an aircraft part and, obviously, no possibility of a man surviving such an impact. Satisfied that they had found enough of Hale, Oliver and Boland to make decent burials, the Germans bulldozed the crater flat.

Right: Looking for ways of identifying the aircraft and the bodies within, German soldiers search the crash site of T1827 UX/H. The river in the background is the Ryå, which flows south past Åbybro and into the fjord. About 100 yards away, out of sight top left, is the wreckage of R3802 UX/A, F/Lt Ellen.

Left: This is all that was left of T1889, John Oates's machine, flown down the village high street and dumped in a field.

The pilots of 5 Staffel/JG77 are saluted by their Gruppenkommandeur, Major Hentschel. (Confusingly, the Luftwaffe term 'Gruppe' corresponds more to an RAF wing, about 35 aircraft, whereas the RAF had two sorts of Group. The fighter group was equated by 'Geschwader', 100+ aircraft; the other was the much larger division of Bomber Command.) From left: Oberfeldwebel (equivalent F/Sgt) Menge, who claimed four Blenheims shot down in the three minutes between 12.15 and 12.18. Next is Feldwebel (Sgt) Petermann, who claimed three Blenheims, times unspecified, then Unteroffizier (also Sgt) Eisseler, two Blenheims at 12.22 and 12.25. Unteroffizier Fröse had one, Gefreiter (Cpl) Brunsmann none, Gefreiter Esser one, Unteroffizier Schmidt two. Not in the picture is the squadron commander, Oberstleutnant (Lt-Col) Friedrich, who claimed two. Total claims fifteen; actual kills, six.

Left: This crew, photographed a few days before Ålborg and replaced on the morning of the raid by Hale and crew, are, from left, Sgt McFarlane, Sgt Eames, P/O Wellings.

Right: As well as the bodies of 82 Squadron men buried here at Vadum, there are four from 102 Squadron, killed in a Whitley bomber 26 April 1940, and six from 10 Squadron, killed in a Halifax bomber 15 October 1944.

Friends reunited: 82 Squadron officers at Oflag 9A, Schloss Spangenberg, an ancient Disney-like castle on a wooded hill. Shortly after the officers left, American bombers flattened it but it was rebuilt in the 1950s and now serves gourmet meals to voluntary guests. From left: P/O Biden, F/Lt Syms, P/O Newland, F/Lt Ellen, F/O McKenzie, P/O Toft, F/Lt Keighley, Sq/Ldr Wardell. All but Toft, McKenzie and Keighley were shot down at Ålborg. Toft's Blenheim was one of the first to go down at Gembloux; he managed to jump before the aircraft exploded in mid-air, but his crew were killed. F/O McKenzie crashed in the Somme on an anti-tank raid, one crew member killed, and F/Lt Keighley came down in the sea off the Dutch coast after trying to find a German target, also one man dead.

Clockwise from top left: John Bristow's POW photograph, taken by the Germans with him clearly in a good mood. Prisoners captured so early in the war faced a long confinement, and many ingenious ways were developed for passing the time in a way that might be productive for the Allied cause. He made all sorts of useful and entertaining objects out of metal scraps and whatever he could find or scrounge off the guards; two of his masterpieces can be seen at the RAF Museum, Hendon.

A good sportsman, Gus Beeby played cricket and football for Ashbourne Grammar School. He joined the RAF in January 1939 and so was one of the many fully trained, professional men that the service could ill afford to lose in those early days of the war. He was shot down over France, but made his way home again, to become the favoured WOp/AG of the new squadron CO, W/C Lart.

Alf Boland, from Hull, flew with several skippers before ending up as Hale's WOp/AG.

In June 1940, George Oliver flew nine ops and married an Exeter girl, Joyce Madge. We don't know the wedding day but Sgt Oliver does seem to have had a week's leave between ops on the 15th and 24th. He joined Earl Hale's crew in July, with Alf Boland in the turret.

Clockwise from top left: Earl Hale, from Saskatchewan, when in RAF training flew his aircraft into the bomb dump. Recovered from massive injuries, he came to 82 Squadron in July 1940.

Ulsterman Bill Magrath would become one of the first Allied airmen to escape from a German POW camp and make it home, but his crash injuries prevented more flying duty so he went into flight control as an officer. He left the RAF as Squadron Leader Magrath MM, and was later Mayor of Salisbury.

John Oates left school at 14 and took a job as an office boy on 12 shillings a week. While learning to fly, he turned a milk round into a sizeable dairy business.

Edmund Lart, the thinking man's Wing Commander, would have realised that his orders to attack Ålborg were the combined result of desperation and muddled tactics. He knew what the chances were, for himself and his squadron, but if he paid any mind to the black day at Gembloux, it didn't deter him. He and his men were at war with the Hun, for King and country, and that was all that mattered.

Clockwise from top left: Thim Biden, observer, was on his first trip with Oates; his experience before this had consisted of three cloudless turn-backs and the cloud-ruined high-level at Haamstede, all with F/Lt Syms.

Norfolk boy Sgt Leslie Youngs, age 21, was observer in Blenheim T1933, the first to go down. He jumped from the aircraft but his parachute failed to open and he was killed instantly on impact.

Tom Girvan, age 19 when he died, WOp/AG with Sq/Ldr Wardell, is seen standing left in a family photo. Brother Hugh served in the army right through the war. Tom was still in training here, yet to earn his aircrew badge and sergeant's stripes.

Bill Greenwood, taken prisoner in 1940, had almost five years in POW camps. This is his ID photo, taken by the Germans. He passed some of the time by writing letters to the Hollywood singing star Deanna Durbin.

Clockwise from top left: Ken Turner, shown here in training, was WOp/AG with Benny Newland in R3904 UX/K, the first machine of A Flight to go down. The pilot was injured but was able to get out of the doomed aircraft. Turner and his observer mate, Yorkshireman George Ankers, were both killed.

Sq/Ldr Norman Jones, pilot of Blenheim T1827 UX/H and leader of the second section of A Flight, was 27 when he was killed at Ålborg, having been with 82 Squadron for three weeks.

For Tom Graham, Ålborg was a baptism of fire. Although he'd been on squadron since the end of June, he had never seen the enemy, nor had his fellow crew members.

P/O Thomas Cranidge, observer in UX/H, was 26 when he died. He was from Crowle, on the Isle of Axholme, north Lincolnshire.

headed for home, but every time we put our nose out of the clouds two Messerschmitts would dive on us.

This must have gone on for about an hour. I really don't know how we got away. At one stage I was firing at a 109 on our starboard quarter, banging away happily although he was really out of range of that rubbish gun, and when I turned to look on the port side there was another 109 about 20 yards away. I could see the pilot quite clearly. I whipped the gun down and fired. I think I hit him but I couldn't swear to it. It all happened so quickly. He didn't fire, so maybe he'd run out of ammo after chasing us for so long. After that we dived down and hedgehopped back to Watton.

These German raids were futile. Each crew was given a specific target but the small loads they could carry were not going to cause much damage, even if they found it and, similarly difficult, hit it. In any case, there were barges gathering in Dutch harbours and the Luftwaffe was populating captured aerodromes in large numbers. The new instructions from RAF HQ were clear, if ambitious: 'The enemy are using airfields and landing grounds in France, Belgium and Holland. The intention is to destroy as many aircraft as possible on the ground thus forcing the enemy to withdraw.'

This order came with a rider: again, aircrew were not to pursue missions if there was insufficient cloud cover. How much cloud was sufficient, and where in the mission the decision to abort should be made, were not specified. Now that the enemy occupied aerodromes on the North Sea and Channel coasts, and was able to expand his Freya radar operation into occupied countries, where was the danger line to be drawn?

CHAPTER SIX

DIFFERENT SORT OF CHAP ALTOGETHER

Strictly speaking, it was not necessary for the officer commanding a squadron to go on operations. Almost all of them did, irregularly rather than frequently, if only to maintain morale, and Paddy Bandon had done that as much as he thought necessary. He was a courageous airman to whom the squadron and the air force meant everything, a good organiser, a formidable opponent, a natural commander, but his main way of keeping spirits up was personal – outgoing, jolly, good for a laugh, good for a pint in the mess, everybody liked him and he liked everybody. That was how he had rebuilt the squadron, through force of personality. His replacement, arriving on 1 July 1940, seemed to be a different kettle of fish – and, at first anyway, a cold one.

Edward Collis de Virac Lart was born in 1902 at Knapp House, Charmouth, Dorset (the house is still there), into a middle class family of French descent. He had two sisters and two brothers. Father, Charles Edmund Lart, served throughout the First World War in the Royal Army Medical Corps and was aged 50 when he came out. He was an author in peacetime, fortunately with private means as his works were not big sellers, with titles such as *Huguenot Pedigrees* (in two volumes) and *The Registers of the Protestant Church at Caen*, and we must admire the dedication that produced *The Parochial Registers of Saint-Germain-en-Laye - Jacobite Extracts of Births, Marriages and Deaths.*

Elder brother Edmund (Ted) lost a leg with the Dorsetshire Regiment in the Great War; younger brother John would join the RAMC like his father and would be killed in January 1944.

Edward went to Weymouth College, today a College of Further Education ('World leaders in Stonemasonry'), then a minor public school, and from his letter home he would appear to be conscious of his own abilities. After St Catharine's, Cambridge, his time at Cranwell overlapped with that of gregarious millionaire Paddy Bandon but we cannot imagine them leading the same social life. They went their separate ways after graduation; Lart was sent on Empire service, to India and Afghanistan, the North West Frontier, and he was there a long time.

His flying machine to begin with was the Airco DH9A, a First World War design still in use through the 1920s and into the 1930s as a general-purpose aircraft and light bomber on Imperial duty. Foreseeing the possibility of a landing on unforgiving ground, it was usual for Lart to carry a spare wheel.

Dear Mother.

I got that shirt. Whatever made you address it to the Junior School. If you address things to Weymouth College it will get there allright. The work in 4B is disgusting stuff which John could easily do. I haven't had half such an bad time as I expected. Will you write and tell me if I can join the O.S.B. We had shooting practice, the other day. There an awful piano to practice on, but Mrs Conway lets me do it on hers. Mr Thom, is an ass; he wanted to put me on to some silly sonata or other, that I learned years ago. If you wrote and told him that I must do some things (I'll send you the no's. of the pages of some nice ones), he'd soon shut up. Please address letters I. Lart.

Much love from
Edward.

Lart Major of 4B seems to think the school isn't working him hard enough. The school piano and the music master leave much to be desired, and as if that wasn't enough, his mother can't even get the address right to send him his new shirts.

The DH9A was succeeded by a like-for-like replacement, the Westland Wapiti. It, too, carried a spare wheel, along with 580lb of bombs, at a cruising speed of 110mph. Top speed was 130mph, slightly quicker than the DH9A. In many cases it could be repaired with the RAF's large stock of DH9A parts, the use of same having been in the design specification.

It was the first aircraft to fly through the Khyber Pass, in 1929 during the RAF's evacuation of some 600 non-Afghan civilians from Kabul, an op that Lart must have been on. The British, after an inconclusive small war with the Afghanis, had recognised their independence in 1919 but the King, Amanullah, introduced European reforms such as education for girls. A civil war resulted, making necessary the evacuation.

Although the last one was built in 1932, the Wapiti was still threading its way through mountain passes in 1940.

Lart found some personal relationships difficult but still waters can run deep. The more extrovert type could misinterpret his taciturn modesty, and class him as stand-offish. His new fellow officers at 82 Squadron certainly thought him a bit of a mystery. The contrast between the two wing commanders, the big, hearty Bandon bear and the slim, ascetic Lart terrier, could hardly have been greater. Knowing Bandon and his reputation, Lart must have been aware of that, but it was not something on which he thought it necessary to comment, nor did he feel the need to recite his history. Consequently, some very odd rumours went about in a bid to explain the sudden arrival of a man who was so different. He must have committed a great indiscretion, or suffered a great personal tragedy, to make him like he was, as if he cared not if he was loved or liked, as if his survival in this war was not a matter of concern.

At this early stage of hostilities, the chaps in the officers' mess were all pre-war regulars and experienced reservists, members of a special club of friends and colleagues whose job it was to kill and avoid being killed and who, off duty, would have chosen for the lesson at Sunday service I Corinthians, chapter 15, verse 32:'If after the manner of men I have fought with beasts at Ephesus, what advantageth it me, if the dead rise not? Let us eat and drink, for tomorrow we die.'

Lart could have quoted those lines as well as anyone, but he let nothing get in the way of his mission, to inflict painful wounds on the enemy with a supremely efficient squadron. The airmen he commanded saw a single-minded, fearless and resolute patrician with a sharp tongue who, some writers have said, was intolerant of, and unsympathetic towards, those ordinary mortals who felt fear, and whose resolution could be undermined by the immediate threat of bullets and flames. If he was chilly and ruthless, as Max Hastings wrote in *Bomber Command*, it was in The Cause. If he was authoritarian, at least he never spared himself from the consequences of his own orders. Of course, those historians never knew him. Here is an extract from a letter to his sister Judith, from his commanding officer overseas, Group Captain Roger Neville MC, a Royal Flying Corps ace with five victories:

Edward served in my squadron in India and again as my adjutant at North Weald. Not only did he show himself to be an able and gallant officer; he was a charming friend to my family; quiet and unassuming in manner yet full of character; and extremely popular with all the right sort of people.

He wrote to me at the beginning of the war, asking whether I could help him to get back from Iraq into an operational squadron. I advised him to wait his turn and told him it would come, I thought, with

Italy's entrance to the war. He is entirely without fear, as far as his brother officers could ever judge, and very determined.

Edward Lart never married but was an excellent substitute elder brother to his CO's son, Christopher (later Air Commodore Neville): 'We spent some memorable holidays together, and my son, who is shortly to enter the RAF himself, has held Edward in the highest esteem as a playmate and companion since they first combined to flout nursery authority fourteen years ago in Kohat.' (Kohat is in modern Pakistan, not far from the Afghan border and the Khyber Pass.)

Relatives who knew Edward Lart describe him as a warm and sociable person; one fellow officer at 82 Squadron had him as austere and uncommunicative. Different people saw different sides of this complex character but there can be no doubting his total commitment to reinventing the squadron after its heart had been ripped out in May, and to defeating Germany at whatever the cost to himself.

Lart came back to Blighty from Iraq as the Germans were smashing their way through the Low Countries and France, seemingly unstoppable. His experience flying biplanes against rebellious tribesmen was not going to contribute much to this war, despite his two mentions in despatches, so he quickly learned to fly Blenheims and went on several ops with another squadron before turning up at No. 82 as the new boss.

Perhaps he felt a little underqualified to be leading these battle-scarred fellows who were flying at the enemy in daylight and suffering losses. Or, more likely, he knew that some of them would think him underqualified, in which case he needed to set an example, to show that he was more than up to it, to earn their respect.

On his second day at the office, twelve of the squadron's Blenheims set off for various industrial targets in Germany; ten came back because there was no cloud cover. One bombed an aerodrome at Gorinchem, east of Rotterdam. Another, tasked with one of the great horror targets of the war, the Dortmund–Ems canal, failed to return, FTR for short. Lart would find out later that his flight commander, Squadron Leader Hurll Fontayne Chester and crew, had hardly crossed the Dutch coast when they were shot down and buried where they fell, at Heerhugowaard, north-east of Alkmaar.

Next day another six went for aerodromes in France and four came back for the usual reason. The two who pressed on to bomb would have been noted by their new CO as made of the right stuff. That Lart himself was constructed of adamantine materials was proved conclusively after a few days of not much happening, when he picked Sgt Beeby to join him in leading another German op. Twelve crews set off to attack industrial targets. There was no cloud cover. Ten turned back, of whom one hit some invasion barges at Rotterdam on the way home. One didn't turn back soon enough and was shot down, while Lart kept going and attacked the aerodrome at Eschwege, 'scoring many hits on aircraft and tarmac'.

This was remarkable for several reasons. Eschwege was a transport and supplies airbase almost exactly in the middle of Germany, about 250 miles from the Dutch coast. All the captains on this mission had had different targets, given as industrial, so presumably Lart was going for something else in central Germany, failed to find it and did the aerodrome instead. He must also have been the only captain to decide that there was sufficient cloud cover to get him there, or perhaps he didn't bother about cloud cover. He couldn't countermand the orders from above, so he could not stop the others from aborting, but he could damn well make his own mind up about pressing on and hope that at least some of the others would get the message.

Gus Beeby in the turret, on his first op since his crash in France less than a month before, and observer F/Sgt Robertson must have wondered if the wingco was always going to want them to fly with him. For Robertson, although it lasted through July, the relationship fortunately for him didn't turn out to be permanent; but Beeby became a fixture.

This op was something of an old boys' reunion, as Sq/Ldr Paddy Delap took with him Sgt Carbutt, 17 May veteran and recent evader, and Sgt Thomas, who had crossed France after 17 May to get home. For Delap it was his last op with 82; he was posted away to head office as wing commander, then group captain. New flight commanders came in. Carbutt and Thomas carried on.

During the month of July, as it became clear that there was indeed a Battle of Britain, the weather prevented the destruction by 2 Group of a great many aircraft on the ground, and the enemy certainly didn't withdraw. The Battle is popularly and rightly seen as a major defensive action, heroically conducted against superior forces by the pilots of Fighter Command, but there was also an offensive side to it, as Bomber Command attacked airfields and invasion preparations, frequently at massive cost.

One date often put forward as the real start of the Battle, although Blenheims had been bombing airfields since mid-June, is 10 July, mainly because it marked the beginning of the Luftwaffe offensive against shipping, when twenty Dornier bombers escorted by forty fighters attacked a convoy off Dover. Five squadrons of Fighter Command set upon them and shot down thirteen at a cost of six (only one pilot killed). There was also a modest raid on Falmouth and Swansea by a flight of Junkers Ju88s without fighter escort, which bombed and returned unmolested.

The less often quoted reason for picking that date was the result of one raid by 2 Group. Six Blenheims of 107 Squadron headed for the aerodrome at Amiens and, as 82 Squadron had experienced back in May, met a ferocious anti-aircraft barrage that hit some and split up the others, ready for attacks by fighters. Five out of the six went down, three crews killed outright, two crews taken prisoner. The flight commander, F/Lt Harold Pleasance, chased by a flock of Me109s, dived to zero feet and zig-zagged for his life across land, dived again over the cliffs to wave-top level, and earned the admiration of the last two following Me109 pilots who waved him a cheery salute as they turned for home.

Meanwhile, Wingco Lart was making his mark. Six went for aerodromes on the 8th; three turned back according to their instructions, Lart and two others did not. The CO was flying almost every op, not including solo weather reccos, but even he turned back on the next one. One machine of the twelve failed to return, P/O Palmer's, crew taken prisoner.

Five out of nine made sure of returning by aborting their venture into Germany on 13 July, one of which was crewed by Earl Hale, George Oliver and Alf Boland on their first trip together, not that such a routine matter would have seemed important at the time. Sergeant Ralston George Oliver joined 82 Squadron as an observer at the end of May 1940 and flew his first op with P/O Percival on the 31st, a dawn raid led by Paddy Bandon to Vleteren and the Pervijze-Diksmuide road. In June he married Joyce and flew nine ops, mostly with P/O Percival. Five more ops with Percival were followed by six with Earl Hale, with Sgt Boland in the turret.

Alf Boland was a jolly sort, the life and soul, keen on dancing and always ready to spend money rather than save it. He did have a regular girlfriend, Mabel, quite a bit younger than him, whom he'd met at a church hall dance. In a telephone call, 12 August 1940, they decided to marry, and they would do that on his next leave.

Earl Robert Hale, farmer's son from Saskatchewan, was born in 1910. Working on the farm stopped being a viable career for a young man during the Depression of the 1930s and he headed west taking any job he could find. He sold sheet music for a while, and worked as a freelance journalist before applying for officer training with the Royal Air Force. By the time war broke out, he was in training in England. He told his local Saskatchewan newspaper that he wasn't sorry he'd come over. 'I'm just another little pin in a little wheel in a big machine and so the best I can do is try not to shear off.'

Posted to 104 training squadron on Blenheims, he came back from a night flight and ran into the bomb dump. The machine was wrecked, two crew had only minor injuries but Hale had a fractured skull and a massive wound across his face. After a spell in hospital he completed his training and joined 82 Squadron in July 1940, where he crewed up with Oliver and Boland, both older 82 Squadron hands by several weeks.

Earl Hale was recruited by the BBC Overseas Service to broadcast on a programme featuring forces personnel from the Empire and Dominions. He sent a telegram home telling his family to be sure to listen in on 11 August. They did listen, and heard the announcer saying that a pilot from Sakatchewan had been due to be on the programme but sorry, he was unavailable.

He was indeed. He was training for a high-level attack on Ålborg.

Of the four who pressed on on 13 July, Lart found his oil refinery and bombed it from 1,000 feet. Sq/Ldr Wardell got lost and arrived home six hours after taking off. One machine was shot down over the sea near the German/Dutch border, one body washed ashore, two never seen again. The other got a little further before also being shot down, WOp/AG killed aged 18, pilot and observer taken prisoner.

A pilot is reported as saying in the mess that he was sick of all this turning back. A colleague pointed out that the ones who didn't turn back tended not to come back at all.

Twelve crews stood by on the 16th to attack aerodromes. Lart took off, presumably too soon to hear the forecast of bad weather that stopped the other eleven, or ignoring it. He, Robertson and Beeby went on their own to St Inglevert, near Calais, where the squadron had been bombing panzers a few weeks before, but now the target was the aerodrome. F/Sgt Robertson got him there but they could see very little through thick mist. Lart had to come in so low to spot any kind of target that he could not release his 250-pounders for fear of blowing himself out of the sky, but he was going to cause some damage, whatever. Dropping a few 40-pounders still ripped some holes in his aircraft. This was the first time that the ground crews had had to repair Lart's self-inflicted wounds, but it would not be the last.

There was a similar story on the 18th, a dawn raid on invasion barges in Dutch waters. Three out of six turned back, one couldn't find the target, and two – including Lart, of course – did what they had gone for.

Over the next few days, 82 Squadron's war consisted mainly of individual flights towards the enemy coast, classed as weather reconnaissances 'with bombing if possible'. On one such recco, a two-hour trip on 23 July, flew a new all-sergeant crew on their first with 82, a team that would eventually have a most remarkable story to tell. Following that recco, they had three turns-back owing to lack of cloud cover and one high-level raid rendered a complete waste of time by too much cloud cover; but their last op was as eventful as it could get. They were Don Blair, pilot, Bill Magrath, observer, Bill Greenwood, WOp/AG.

Wingco Lart didn't go on these weather-recco trips, but as soon as orders came in to attack Germany he was there. The policy was still to give each crew a separate target, with the usual instructions not to carry on without cloud cover.

With hindsight, we can ask what was the point? They rarely found these targets even if they did carry on. If they did bomb, they caused little damage, so the net result of 82 Squadron's efforts in July 1940 was almost no pain inflicted on the enemy for the loss of six aircraft and crews. That it was not seven was down to the flying skills of Edward Lart and, we can suggest, the gunnery of Gus Beeby.

Four Blenheims had set off for industrial targets in Germany. Three turned back. Lart, as ever, found it almost impossible to leave an operation without trying to do something useful, so he bombed Leeuwarden aerodrome. As he headed for home he was attacked by four Me109s. ORB: 'He shook them off and returned to Watton, his port undercarriage collapsing on landing. There were several bullet holes in his machine. The crew were uninjured.'

They were away again four days later, twelve Blenheims with their thousand-pound loads, all with individual targets in Germany. Just three got there, skippers Ellen, Hale and Wellings, and bombed. Three including Lart bombed shipping and an aerodrome in The Netherlands on the way back, five turned back, and one, skipper F/Lt Keighley, didn't come back at all.

Next day they were after the aerodromes in France, Belgium and Holland. Fordham, with Carbutt and Thomas, was chased by several Me109s that shot up the port engine and put bullet holes in many places, but Sgt Thomas claimed one Messerschmitt down before they escaped into cloud and limped home. Lart, naturally, 'bombed his target successfully' and only three out of the twelve found the cloud cover so insufficient that they turned back. Was there a Lart Effect?

July ended with another trip to Germany, mostly ineffective, although Canadian P/O Earl Hale, now with two weeks' experience, had an exciting time being chased by two fighters, Me109 and He113 according to the ORB, for 35 minutes, starting five miles north of Amsterdam. The pursuit was mostly at wave-top level after Hale dived from 6,000 feet. WOp/AG Sgt Alf Boland claimed the Messerschmitt, shot down into the sea as it turned away from an attack; the other fighter appeared to run out of ammunition and give up.

That Hale was chased cannot be doubted; that one of the chasers was the He113 is impossible, because such an aircraft did not exist. For reasons that are not apparent, unless it was purely for propaganda, the Germans took many photographs of a failed Heinkel design of a single-seater and portrayed it as the new super-fighter that was equipping the Luftwaffe in large numbers. The British certainly believed this, publishing aircraft identification charts and never doubting its mention in combat reports, as here with 82 Squadron, but never wondering why – despite all the claims by RAF fighter pilots in 1940 to have shot one down – no example of this machine was ever found.

So, Hale was chased by two Me109s but he got away, which was all that mattered, and he landed at Watton with no undercarriage in a machine full of holes. With cloud cover lacking, most of the rest of the twelve bombed secondary targets along the coast while one pilot flew right into the heart of the Ruhr and beyond. Unable to spot his industrial target, Wingco Lart bombed Paderborn aerodrome instead.

Hardly surprisingly, Lart's persistence and example-setting had been noticed at HQ. He had flown more ops – and very dangerous ones too – in a single month than most squadron COs might be expected to fly in a year. The Air Officer Commanding 2 Group, Air Commodore James Robb, put the wingco's name forward for the DSO – Distinguished Service Order, at this time only awarded to those already mentioned in despatches, and to officers only, usually fairly senior officers (major in the army, squadron leader in the air force and above), unless it was for a truly exceptional act of bravery that, for some reason, didn't quite merit the Victoria Cross. Lart's citation stated: 'By his courage, devotion to duty and skill as a pilot he has set an inspiring example which has more than maintained the excellent esprit de corps of all ranks under his command.'

The award was not made public for some time, so Gus Beeby in the turret and F/Sgt Robertson in the observer's office could not have known that their skipper had been recommended for the second-top gong, and we can only speculate whether they might have occasionally wished for a little less of the inspiring example and a bit more of the turning back.

During that month of July in 2 Group, an average of one Blenheim a day failed to return, plus three that did return but would never fly again. Of the 93 missing crew, 58 were dead. It was against this background that Edward Lart, the allegedly chilly and ruthless commander, more than maintained the fighting spirit of his squadron.

With the Battle of Britain now raging, Hurricanes and Spitfires in a desperate struggle, pilots flying several ops a day, the question was – to what use could 82 Squadron's fighting spirit be put? Blenheims couldn't fly as defensive fighters. They'd have had no chance. No, the only thing they could do that would help in this last-ditch attempt to repel a German invasion was to bomb the Luftwaffe on the ground. The Commander-in-Chief of Bomber Command, Air Marshal Portal, ordered more attacks on enemy airfields; forget about Germany for the moment, but don't press home the attacks without fighter escorts and/or cloud cover.

There were no fighters to spare for escorting jobs, and if there was no cloud then 2 Group could not contribute a penn'orth of damage to the enemy. One idea was to try high-level bombing instead, 20,000 feet, of the kind later practised at night by 500 Lancasters at a time, each carrying ten times a Blenheim load. There were several reasons why this was unlikely to work.

The aircraft, the Blenheim, was not a good flyer at that height. The much more nimble German fighters would have an even greater advantage than normal, so close formation flying would be even more important, and more difficult. Secondly, there was no bombsight that could be expected to work accurately at 20,000 feet so a crew had very little chance of hitting the target with their one thousand pounds of bombs.

Thirdly, there was Freya. Although individual sorties did little damage, at least they were not likely to cause great concern at the German radar stations, the effectiveness of which was still not fully appreciated by the British. Large formations flying high would be spotted in plenty of time to organise a hostile reception.

Nevertheless, 82 Squadron was ordered to train in these new tactics and spent the first five days of August doing so. John Bristow: 'We were told we had to do a high-level bombing raid so, for a few days, we went up to 20,000 feet, which in those days was considered very high, and got used to wearing our oxygen masks.'

This training was interrupted on the 6th by an orthodox attack on aerodromes, when twelve of the thirteen turned back, including Bristow with his new pilot, newcomer flight commander Sq/Ldr Norman Jones. One did not turn back, bombing the Luftwaffe base at Boulogne and, when he got home, Lart again had to order his ground crew to repair some damage he'd done to his machine by going in so low. England and the wing commander expected every man to do his duty, but there didn't seem to be so many who would ignore the cloud-cover orders.

Maybe things would be better the next day, when twelve of the same crews who had set off yesterday were to try out the new high-level style of raid. The target was the aerodrome at Haamstede, on an island between Vlissingen (Flushing) and Rotterdam. They flew in two boxes of six, one led by Jones with Bristow in the turret, one by Lart. When they got there, they found so much cloud cover that they couldn't see a thing from 20,000 feet and came home without bombing, except for P/O Wellings who had a go on his own. If he did any damage it is not recorded.

This would not have been classed as a real trial of the idea. It just so happened that it would have been a much better day for the normal kind of raid they'd been doing, and maybe they could have bombed Haamstede from low level without having to turn back. If high-level raids were to be tested as a way of getting better results with less risk, another target would have to be found and another day assigned and, as 82 Squadron was doing all this training, they would be the obvious outfit for the job.

Meanwhile there was another standard op, nine went to airfields, six came back early, one hit Cherbourg, one hit Guernsey (the undefended islands of Jersey and Guernsey had been occupied 30 June/1 July) and one failed to return.

That was on the 10th. We don't know exactly when British Intelligence concluded that many aircraft, bombers and troop carriers were massing at Ålborg in Denmark, ready for the invasion of Britain, but the orders came in to Wing Commander Lart on the afternoon of the 12th. He was to mount a high-level raid on Tuesday the 13th, irrespective of cloud cover and from 20,000 feet, 'if possible'. The attack was to be pressed home at all costs.

In fact, the German bombers were being collected for *Adler Tag*, Eagle Day, also the 13th, when the Luftwaffe was to launch a great offensive against RAF airfields. In any case, regardless of why there were scores of Ju88s there, Ålborg aerodrome would be very well defended.

Ålborg, an ancient trading port on the Limfjord but by this time a major industrial centre and the third city of Denmark, opened its new airport in May 1938. When

German paratroopers landed there on the evening of 9 April, the intention was to make it a forward base for the Luftwaffe as an aid to conquering Norway and a refuelling facility on Germany–Norway–Germany flights. Being designed only for use by small civilian aircraft on intra-Scandinavian business, it was nowhere near adequate for the Germans. However, the site was excellent, and all that was in the way were a couple of hundred farms and homesteads and a manor house.

By 26 July, every obstruction had been demolished and three concrete runways built, largely with Danish forced labour. When those large numbers of aircraft began to assemble there, to add to the interest already focused on the place by British Intelligence due to the refuelling activity, Ålborg became a high priority.

CHAPTER SEVEN

AT ALL COSTS, IF POSSIBLE

All the paradoxes and contradictions in such a raid would have been obvious to a man like Lart. The idea of flying at 20,000 feet was to put his men and machines out of danger from the flak, which it might to a certain extent, but the threat from fighters would be increased because of the Blenheim's sluggish performance at that height. There was virtually no possibility of bombing accurately from there, and even the slightest hope of hitting the target would depend on crews being able to see clearly, so cloud that might hide them from the enemy would also prevent them from doing their job. Sunny skies would mean them being spotted in plenty of time for a hot reception to be prepared, and they had no escorts to give them a fighting chance.

There was no instruction about turning back on this one. They were to press on regardless of cloud cover. The proviso about bombing from 20,000 feet 'if possible' only took Lart back to the beginning again. What would make it possible? Clear skies. What would clear skies do? Make them sitting ducks. John Bristow:

> We were called to the briefing room and told we were going to bomb Ålborg, in Jutland, where there was a lot of German aircraft and a fighter base. We were also told that the flight there was 450 miles, so that made Ålborg a little bit past the loaded Blenheim's range so we probably wouldn't get back to Watton. We were to make for an airfield in Scotland or anywhere we could. Whatever we did, we were told 'Don't use Boost Nine, because if you use Boost Nine you will not have enough petrol to get back to anywhere.'
>
> My first thought was that we'll force-land in Sweden and have a week's holiday. Most of the rest thought this was a silly mission, to bomb a place where we already knew the fighters were there.

There was indeed a fighter base but, according to the latest information, it was temporarily unoccupied. *Gefreiter* (Corporal) Heinrich Brunsmann, a pilot with 5 Staffel of *Jagdgeschwader* 77 (Luftwaffe approximate equivalent to a squadron of a fighter group) had an intriguing theory about why the RAF decided to attempt the Ålborg raid on the day they did:

> Quite near to the Ålborg fighter base [Rørdal aerodrome, also known as Ålborg Ost] was a cement

factory that in peacetime was owned by a British company. Not known at the time but later discovered, certain workers at the factory were acting as agents for British Intelligence, transmitting information about the comings and goings at the several aerodromes. On the morning of 12 August, 1 Staffel of our group left the Ålborg base and so it would have appeared to the agents to be ungarrisoned, and this would have been reported by radio immediately. Somehow, the same agents failed to notice our arrival (5 Staffel) in the evening, so when the English squadron attacked Ålborg next day, nobody would have reckoned with there being a German fighter squadron ready to defend it.

If Corporal Brunsmann is right, either that information never reached 2 Group or, if it did, it was withheld from Wing Commander Lart. If it was in fact passed on, he chose not to include it in his briefing. The latter case is surely impossible to believe, and it cannot have been reasonable for Group not to relay such encouraging news, so we are left with the most likely explanation. The agents' information, false anyway, if it was ever transmitted, got stuck somewhere and 82 Squadron went on their operation believing the truth: that there were fighters waiting for them.

Whatever their individual feelings, it was the belief at least of *The Times* Aeronautical Correspondent that here were men with a mission. That was the phrase he used, under the headline 'Changed outlook of RAF pilots and gunners', and the change he put down to aircrew seeing the indiscriminate slaughter of refugees and other civilians, and of shipwrecked sailors, by the Luftwaffe. Of course, 82 Squadron had seen plenty of attacks on refugees in France and Belgium and we can be sure that such sights hardened hearts, but we can doubt if the boys would have recognised themselves in this description:

> In the early months, flying for these young men in blue was a gay adventure; it was, to use a popular RAF expression, 'grand fun'. Now all this has changed. From being daring young adventurers of the air they have become Men With A Mission, men who feel a personal responsibility to destroy that threatening machine which is the Luftwaffe. Gone are the young men who flew for the thrill it gave them, and in their place are the cold-eyed, determined pilots and air gunners bent upon the destruction of their foe.

Cold-eyed or no, take-off was scheduled for 08.40. The load was the usual four 250lb high-explosive bombs plus eight small fragmentation bombs, which were 25lb of explosive and shrapnel that worked as anti-personnel mines and, hopefully, might rip a few holes in parked aircraft.

There were delays. One was caused by the accidental opening of a parachute, when Ronald Ellen's observer Sgt John Dance, in his hurry to get aboard, snagged the metal ring that does the job. Parachute training in Bomber Command consisted of showing you how to put the pack on, and what to pull once you were clear of the aircraft. There were no practice jumps. Every airman's first experience of a jump was the one he made to escape from doom, and so every airman climbed into his machine hoping, maybe believing, that he wouldn't need this inconvenient parcel he had to lug around. Sgt Dance said something to the effect of having to manage without one. F/Lt R A G 'Nellie' Ellen told him to go and get another, sharpish.

The clerk was opening the day's mail and found something from HQ that was of fateful importance. P/O Don Wellings, Sgt Don McFarlane and Sgt Peter Eames were posted elsewhere and so their place on the op was taken by the crew on stand-by, George Oliver and Alf Boland skippered by Earl Hale. And so off they went, twelve aircraft and crews, bound for Jutland. Sergeant John Oates in UX/L was Lart's port wingman.

John Oates left school at 14, as so many did then, for a job as office boy on twelve shillings a week. After two years, he and his sister took on a milk round turning over £23 a week. That was in 1925 and by 1940 John had a sizeable dairy retail business and had moved into making butter and cream.

Meanwhile he had learned to fly, at Hamble near Southampton, and later joined the RAF Volunteer Reserve through the Doncaster Aero Club, near his home. When the war began, he trained as a fighter pilot and, despite (or because of) being classed as above average, was transferred to two engines and the Blenheim, much to his disgust. Posted to 18 Squadron, lately back from France as an army Air Component, he was transferred to 82 and flew his first op with them 2 July, the one on which his flight commander,

Sq/Ldr Chester, failed to return. Oates: 'At this early stage of the war, we flew single intruder flights in daylight and were briefed to turn back if there was no cloud cover. I became an expert at gentle landings with bombs still attached.'

Today there was no turning back.

'We crossed the North Sea at 5,000 feet flying just above ten tenths cloud, but that cleared before the Danish coast. We divided into our two flights as we neared the target.' Bill Magrath:

'As I always did, I ate all my chocolate ration before take-off, not wishing to waste any of it in the event of being shot down. We were to set course for the western mouth of the Limfjorden and follow that up to the target. It was a fine day at Watton, but there was thick cloud over the sea. We went up to 8,000 feet when we reached the Danish coast and split up into our flights. My crew was in B Flight, which was Sq/Ldr Wardell's.'

The formation was four sections of three in vic (an inverted V made of one in front and two behind and to either side, stepped down). Lart was in the lead, with Oates and Wigley port and starboard wingmen behind, then came Sq/Ldr Jones leading his section of Ellen and Newland. B Flight had Rusty Wardell in front, with Baron and Hale wingmen, then F/Lt Syms leading Blair (observer Magrath) and Parfitt. Magrath:

'We saw the cloud was disappearing as we reached the coast, and that our leader's navigator had made a mistake. We were some way south of where we should have been, coming in at Ringkøbing.'

Elsewhere it has been suggested that there was no mistake

and the wingco had decided on a different, more direct route, to save fuel, rather than go up to the fjord mouth. Looking at the map of Denmark, we can see that there is a difference in the two flight paths. Making landfall at Ringkøbing, the distance across the sea might have been slightly less but there remained around 110 miles to go across Jutland, giving the Germans – once messages had been received and understood – half an hour to prepare their reception. From the fjord mouth at Thyborøn to Ålborg is about 70 miles, giving the enemy less time but, surely, still an ample amount.

It has also been said that the mistake was due to the inexperience of the observer/navigator, twenty-two-year-old Pilot Officer Maurice Gillingham, who replaced the long serving Flight Sergeant Robertson in Lart's crew because the wingco preferred having an officer. It is certainly true that Gillingham had had only one previous op with 82 Squadron, the abortive high-altitude raid on Haamstede, when he flew with Lart while Robertson went with Nellie Ellen. However, there were other officer observers on the squadron and, if Lart had been minded that way, he would surely have picked one of them before this point. He had flown with Robertson all through July, which was three flights into Germany and six into occupied countries, which suggests that the wing commander was more than satisfied with the flight sergeant's navigating. Indeed, there were two officer observers in other aircraft on the Ålborg op. More probable is that Robertson was due some leave and Lart felt that, having taken the novitiate to Haamstede, he should stick with young Gillingham rather than find a more experienced sergeant.

He was also sticking with the same machine. This was the fourth in a row flying T1934 UX/R, which is curious because there was no culture of 'my' aircraft in the squadron, unlike some squadrons flying Wellingtons or Hampdens, for instance, where crews who lasted long enough became attached to one particular aircraft. In later days, when the larger Lancaster and Halifax crews formed a kind of affection for 'their' aircraft, they often renamed it and added a nose painting, 'Willing Winnie' or 'Lonesome Lola'. In 82 Squadron, crews were randomly assigned to aircraft and never did the several consecutive ops in Z-Zebra or S-Sugar that would have been necessary to build up some sort of possessive feeling.

By the time they reached the coast, Sgt Norman Baron had broken radio silence to tell Lart that his gauges were showing low fuel. Perhaps the gauges were faulty; more likely there really was something wrong in the fuel system. In any case, he informed the wingco that, as was proper procedure, he was turning back and Lart could not order him to stay.

There was a Freya radar station on that coast, which could not estimate the flying height of invaders but could tell distance and direction, and which had often been in work in previous weeks when Bomber Command was raiding at night. Reports from this newfangled and temperamental machine had been questioned before, when its signals indicated attackers in broad, cloudless daylight. Why would the Tommies come on a beautiful summer's day like this? Were they mad, or suicidal?

As those Tommies crossed into Denmark, they were also spotted the old-fashioned way, by the watchers at the Søndervig lookout post. So, there was plenty of information to suggest that the English bombers must be going for Ålborg; there were no other worthwhile targets, no other enemy installations that could justify the risk of a raid in bright sunshine. John Bristow: 'The wing commander was obviously hoping that the cloud cover would stretch all the way to Ålborg but directly we hit the coast, at the wrong place, well down south, the clouds went. The wingco decided to carry on, and he had the authority so we had to carry on too, a hundred miles across enemy-occupied Denmark without a cloud in the sky.'

Ålborg aerodrome was very important to the Germans. Eagle Day would be the beginning of the end for Britain. It was intended that the Ju88 bombers would have fighter escorts to make sure they did what was required, but the fighters stationed at the subsidiary field, Ålborg Ost, arrived from Norway the evening before, had defence of the main aerodrome as their primary task. When word came through that the British bombers were on their way, the eight fighters of 5 Staffel/Jagdgeschwader 77 were scrambled, to climb to attack height and wait.

The normal strength of a staffel was twelve, made up of pairs called *Rotte,* (pack, as in hounds) each fielding a *Rottenführer* and a *Katschmarek* (wingman). While stooging about waiting for their prey, the eight available Me109s of 5 Staffel would have been flying in their pairs, a couple of hundred yards apart. In a dogfight with Spitfires or Hurricanes, the wingman was expected to prevent the enemy getting on his leader's tail, as well as looking after himself, a case of *quis custodiet ipsos custodes* (who shall guard the guardians?) if ever there was one. There was also the tactical option of the *Schwarm* (flock, flight), two *Rotten* in a flat, stepped-back formation led by the most experienced and capable pilot rather than the most senior in rank.

As the Blenheims were without fighter escort, these German pilots might not have been expecting to have to resort to tactics.

Whatever Lart thought about their chances of survival, he knew very well that their only chance of inflicting serious damage on the enemy was to go in low. From 20,000 feet 'if possible', even if they'd had the petrol to get there, there was no hope of hitting the target except by pure luck. From 8,000 feet, where they now were, hopes were obviously better but still slim. So, he began a steady descent to 3,000 feet, followed by the rest of A Flight.

Rusty Wardell did something similar, except he led his five of B Flight, minus Baron, a little way off to starboard, planning to come at the drome from a different direction, thus to give the anti-aircraft gunners something else to think about.

As at Gembloux, the German defenders' stratagem was straight-forward. Put up a flak barrage, scatter the Tommies, and let the fighters pick off the survivors. The difference here was the Ålborg flak establishment, permanent rather than mobile, was highly professional and thoroughly drilled, well set up to guard the approaches to the city and, more importantly, the airfield to the north-east, beyond the city, over the waters of the fjord.

A Flight still had six miles or so to the target when the flak opened up. No major hurts were suffered as they pressed on, the outlying gunners seemingly not yet finding their range quite accurately enough. Well, they would make sure they were in better order when the next lot of Englanders tried their luck. Meanwhile, A Flight reached the aerodrome where more flak and the fighters awaited them.

In the turret of Blenheim T1889 UX/L was Sergeant Tom Graham, who had crewed with Oates since they came to the squadron in late June. They'd had six ops together, two of them solo weather reccos and four cloudless turns-back lasting a couple of hours at most. Oates had done one more op with a different WOp/AG but that had been a turn-back too. Their usual observer, the experienced Sgt Hutcherson, who had come onto squadron back in May, after Gembloux, had been transferred, making room for Thim Biden, which made three who had never seen the enemy. Sergeant John Oates, pilot:

Flying at number two in A Flight I saw nothing of the action but could hear plenty, then a few seconds after bombing we were hit by flak in the turret and knocked over. As we fell I realised the machine could still fly so I let it fall to near the ground. Thim [P/O Biden, observer, flying with Oates for the first time] thought we were going to crash and was getting ready to bale out. Our intercom was u/s after the turret was hit so all I could do was reach down to tap him with my foot and hope he understood my signal. As soon as we levelled out we were hit by the fighters, and with no intercom I was getting no news about where they were from gunner or observer. All we could do was fly on as close to the ground as we could.

Oates had dropped his bombs somewhere on the airfield, as had the others of A Flight, but what made the difference in their fates was that Oates's enforced solo low flying allowed him to escape the further attentions of the fighters, while the other five, reassembling in their formation behind their leader, to the German eye looked the easier and potentially more fruitful option.

Although the damage to the aerodrome was not great and would soon be repaired, the crews of A Flight did manage to hit the target with some bombs bang in the middle, and that despite immense pressure from ground fire. Oates's machine was the only one badly damaged but all of A Flight took hits from the airfield guns.

For a brief moment, the men of A Flight were free and speeding north-west.

Now there was a new objective for the German flak gunners. B Flight arrived in close formation, five Blenheims together making a textbook target. This time, the outlying flak batteries made no mistake.

The first hits on Doug Parfitt's Blenheim, T1933 UX/C, flying starboard wingman to F/Lt Syms, were bad enough but not sufficient to bring him down. He jettisoned his bombs to give himself more of a chance, and they fell in a field killing some cattle, while he faced a rather difficult choice. One, try to stay in formation and go through more flak, two, abandon ship, three, turn away and run, knowing that there were bound to be fighters about. There were eight 109s in the air; two pairs had gone after A Flight while the others hung around to see what leftovers there might be from the anti-aircraft barrage.

For Parfitt, such considerations became irrelevant very quickly. The third choice – to flee – was not really an option anyway, and we can speculate that he had come to Decision Two and given the order to jump seconds before a direct hit on the tail blew the whole of that section off. Only the observer, Les Youngs, had been able to get out before, we conclude, simply because it is hard to see how he could have done that from a tail-less aircraft plunging to the ground at terrific speed.

Certainly the other two men were trapped, and poor Les Youngs could not profit from his early release, as his chute didn't open and he was killed just the same. A local man, carpenter E A Madsen, saw the fall and went to investigate. He was deeply moved to find the body and sat there a while, noticing the name on the unopened parachute pack. Mr Madsen would have been even more affected had he known that this had been twenty-one-year-old Leslie Youngs's first operation – as indeed it had been for WOp/AG Ken Neaverson, killed in the crash, and only his third for the skipper, likewise dead.

And then there were four Bs, still with some way to go to the target: Wardell and Hale up front, Syms and Blair following. Parfitt's section leader, F/Lt T E Syms in R3800 UX/Z took a hit that turned his aircraft right over. Syms was a regular from before the war but a very recent arrival at 82 Squadron, flying four ops since late July, none of which had resulted in contact with the enemy. He was more than making up for it now, and wasted no time in telling his crew to get out and did so himself. Sergeant K H Wright did likewise, and for a moment it seemed that his jump would be in vain as he dropped through a burst of machine gun bullets, he thought aimed at him. While parachuting airmen, obviously trained for war operations, were generally considered fair game, in that shooting them would prevent them reappearing on another occasion, it must be unlikely that a fighter pilot in the midst of the battle would have had the time or inclination to fire at one man when there were several nice fat Tommy aircraft left to knock down. We must conclude that Sergeant Wright happened to be in the way of more important business.

In any case, he was unharmed and landed fairly gently in the shallow water of the Limfjord shore, close to where his skipper had recently been met by courteous German soldiers who helped him limp to the beach with a broken ankle. Wright, like his skipper, was not asked to make it to the shore alone. The WOp/AG, Sergeant Edward Turner, age twenty, was in the aircraft when it crashed, perhaps dead already, more likely wounded by the flak or unable to escape for some other reason. Flight Sergeant Bill Magrath was the observer in R2772 UX/T:

> We were hit by the flak on our bombing run and the port engine was on fire. We got shot of our bombs only to find we were under attack from fighters. I got down on the floor of the nose-blister and fired the under-gun, which was a Browning machine gun that nobody expected to do any good,

but at least it was a contribution, and my reward was a bullet in the leg from a Messerschmitt. We were full of holes from the flak and the fighters were adding more. It didn't look like we could stay in the air much longer.

Pilot Sergeant Don Blair thought so too, and attempted a crash-landing-cum-ditching in the fjord, close to the shore of Egholm island. This might have been a good plan but an explosion in one wing dropped them suddenly, at a point where the shallow water covered large and sharp rocks. The aircraft was wrecked completely and all its crew suffered bad injuries. Magrath, hip and a shoulder broken and blinded in one eye, lay semi-conscious. Greenwood, who had fared slightly better than the others but still had an ankle shot through and broken in three places, saw his captain in such a bloody mess that he thought he must be dead.

Danes who had watched the catastrophic end of R2772 waded out expecting to find three bodies and instead had the problem of moving men alive who clearly were in no state to be moved. While some prepared the nearest thing they had to an ambulance, a bed of loose straw on a farm cart, others carried the airmen to this relatively luxurious transport. From there they would be driven slowly and gently across the island to the quay used by the Ålborg ferry, and thence to the German-occupied hospital in the city.

The stand-by crew, the last minute replacements, were led by Earl Hale. The Canadian had escaped from two Me109s when he last encountered fighters but he could see no possibility of getting out of his current fix. Although damaged by flak he had pressed on and reached the target, to meet fire from gunners below and fighters above that was surely too much for any aircraft.

It was certainly too much for R3821 UX/N. Although right on the spot and, as it were, with an open goal, no bombs fell from UX/N. Perhaps, having got this far, they thought they might as well try and hit the biggest building they could see, which was the station HQ.

Whatever came first, the death of the pilot or the shooting away of the last bit of flying ability from the aircraft, R3821 smashed into the airfield with all bombs aboard and exploded, digging a crater 15 feet deep and more. Nobody watching could have imagined even the slightest possibility of a man surviving such a complete disintegration.

Hale had been sticking close to his leader, B Flight commander Rusty Wardell, who had dropped his bombs and somehow run through the hot metal curtain that had downed his wingman. The fate of R3829 was not long postponed, because Wardell was carrying with him the fire started by the flak shells back at the aerodrome. Soon the cockpit was ablaze and the pilot was being burned alive. He called his order to jump and, despite the pain of his seared face and hands, got out himself. One crewman was unable to move, dead or wounded. One did make the attempt but by then he was too near the ground. He tried to deploy the chute anyway, the cords and silk became tangled around the aircraft's tail and he was dragged down.

The resulting explosion was so great that there was no

immediate prospect of telling which of the charred bodies had been in the machine and which one had been tied to it, and the evidence was lost.

Flight Sergeant George Moore, observer, was a thirty-year-old regular from pre-war days, a married man. He and WOp/AG Tom Girvan, nineteen years old, had been Wardell's crew since the squadron leader had joined the squadron in late June as a flight lieutenant.

So, that was the whole of B Flight gone, with nine men dead and six more very lucky not to be. The fighters closed in on the five aircraft of A Flight. Sgt John Bristow was Sq/Ldr Norman Jones's observer in Blenheim T1827 UX/H, section leader behind Lart:

'We'd had the flak all around us and we'd taken a lot of shrapnel. We'd dropped our bombs and tried to run, then the fighters closed in. I saw my best friend Beeby go down in flames, who was with the wing commander.' (Bristow is mistaken in this; he saw somebody go down but Lart, Gillingham and Beeby had a way to go yet.)

Sgt Oates being out of the reckoning on his hedge-hop to safety, the Me109 pilots naturally picked on the tail-enders first, and Newland in R3904 UX/K was lagging. Flak damage was slowing him down and, like the weakest animal in the herd, the lions picked him out.

Benjy Newland did not have his usual crew. His regular WOp/AG, Sgt Herbert Doughty, was on leave, and Sgt Turner had been with this skipper only once before Ålborg, a solo venture to Gelsenkirchen spoiled by the weather, with afterthought bombing of a Dutch aerodrome.

Bullets riddled the machine. One went through Newland's shoulder. More wounded or killed his crewmen, Ken Turner in the turret and George Ankers up front. There was very little possibility in a crippled Blenheim of any crew member helping another who was disabled. Newlands could do nothing for his men, except give the order to jump and struggle himself, one-handed, with his cockpit canopy.

His parachute landed him near the little town of Åbybro, then home to 1,000 people, about 5 miles north-east of the target. He would reconvene with some of his 82 Squadron colleagues in Oflag 9, Schloss Spangenberg, more or less in the centre of Germany. Sgt Doughty would come back to Watton to find himself slated to fly with a new skipper on the 15th, but missing Ålborg only postponed his fortune (see Postscript).

Squadron Leader Norman Jones, replacement flight commander for Hurll Chester, had flown his first op with 82 Squadron on 24 July, an innocuous dawn weather recco, with old hand John Bristow in the turret and new boy P/O Tom Cranidge as observer. They did five more ops together before this one, with Jones leading the second section of A Flight, behind Lart's, although the second section now was down to two. In came the fighters.

John Bristow was very busy indeed in his turret, wondering how on earth he was supposed to achieve the maker's specified firing rate of 1,200 rounds a minute, which would mean changing his 100-round pans every five seconds, and since he was only carrying a little more than a specified minute's worth of ammo, and the combined firing rate of three Me109s was almost incalculable, and however many rounds he shot off at the bastards it didn't seem to make any difference … Bristow: 'Running was not likely to be a great success when really all we had was a single and not very good machine gun in the turret and a single and probably useless rear-firing one under the nose. Against that, we had a 109 underneath and behind us, another above and behind us, and one coming in on the starboard beam, all much faster and with cannon as well as machine guns.'

The Blenheim had no chance. It was when, not if, the ever-increasing number of bullets and holes became terminal. Surprisingly, considering the sheer volume of munitions directed at his aircraft, Bristow's part of it was still more or less entire.

We were soon on fire. I was blasting away at our pursuers, and I turned to the front to see what had happened. Normally, I'd be able to see the heads of the pilot and the observer but they weren't there. There was no reply on the intercom so I had to assume they had been killed in the fighters' attack. Now the port wing was really ablaze and we were going down fast, from not very high up.

Flying with the section leader meant we had the camera, which was fitted over the emergency escape hatch underneath my turret, so to get out I had to unship the camera first. Then I could kick out the hatch, clip on my parachute and dive through the hole.

John Bristow had nature against him. The wind and the G-force caused by the almost vertical, high-speed dive made a clear jump impossible and he was swung back from whence he came.

'My feet were trapped and I was being pressed hard against the outside of the fuselage. I could not move at all, no matter how much I tried to push myself away with one hand, while I kept hold of my chute ripcord with the other.'

Bristow had not had the foresight of Bill Magrath and still carried his chocolate ration. Even in this desperate situation, he could still feel severe disappointment as the wind sucked the chocolate pack from his pocket. As it zipped past his face, he did have cause for thanks for a different kind of foresight:

> I always had my boots undone, thinking that we might ditch in the sea and I'd need to get rid of them quickly. Just as I lost my chocolate ration, hoping that some Danish children might find it rather than a German soldier, I came free of my boots and the aircraft. As it hurtled on to crash a moment later, I pulled my ripcord and floated down on one of the shortest parachute journeys ever. I can't have been more than five or six hundred feet up when I pulled that cord, because I landed literally seconds later.

The fighters' attack on Bristow's Blenheim was almost simultaneous with their similarly fatal destruction of Nellie Ellen's, R3802 UX/A, port wingman of A Flight's rear section. Ellen himself was unscathed but his aircraft was out of control and falling fast. The turret had taken a thumping, so there was no intercom. He could only make wild gestures at his observer, John Dance, to jump, remembering that this was the man who had been willing, in the scramble to take off, to fly without a chute. Sergeant Dance remembered that as he rolled out of the front hatch.

Ellen couldn't see anything of his WOp/AG, Gordon Davies. Either he was dead on the floor or he'd made his own decision and gone. The pilot's hatch was stuck tight and there was no time to wrestle with it. Ellen slid down and out through the nose, pulled his ripcord and landed in a bog. A moment later, somebody else did the same. Maybe it was Taffy Davies. John Bristow:

'I actually landed right beside Flight Lieutenant Ellen, who said hello like we were meeting in the pub, and produced a little flask of whisky. I didn't think that was in the King's Regulations but we had a drink anyway. Just then, a farm worker came running up to us, and we asked him how we could get away and back to England. He didn't understand the words but he got the message and led us to a barn.'

Two left now, as far as the fighter pilots knew. Like Jones and Ellen before them, Clive Wigley in R3913 UX/M, and Edward Lart in T1934 UX/R, were subject to the Germans' full attention at more or less the same time. The two crews knew what had already happened behind them. They knew exactly what to expect next. The WOp/AGs, Archie Morrison and Gus Beeby, would have been describing on the intercom the awful slaughter happening not many yards away. As Jones's and Ellen's machines went down, with three parachutes between them, those six men, all that seemingly remained of the Ålborg raid, must have been fully aware of their fate. It was their turn.

Wigley, observer Sergeant Arthur Patchett and Morrison had done one op with 82 Squadron, and that was a no-cloud turn-back three days before, against Dutch aerodromes. Danish aerodromes were obviously very different. In view of the pilot's inexperience, Lart presumably had Wigley as his starboard wingman so he could look after the young man.

They were some 25 miles beyond the target and with the coast in sight, when volley after volley crashed through their aircraft. It is not known who was killed then and who died in the crashes, but there were no parachutes this time. The wrecks of the two planes were within a mile of each other in the Klithuse area, one in the woods, Wigley's, the other in a field. When Dr Christensen of Brovst hospital came out in the afternoon to inspect the remains, he found that Lart's crash had been so violent that only one body could be identified, that of observer Maurice Gillingham.

Where was John Oates the while? With his turret knocked out by flak he had no defences apart from the famous under-gun, and no wireless to ask for bearings or to contact base. He had no intercom, so the crew couldn't talk. Although he had escaped the fighters by his hedge-hopping, he was carrying the extra damage they had inflicted to add to the holes punched by the flak. Oates:

By the time we crossed the coast we were in bad shape. The port engine was only partly serviceable, we had big holes in the wings, and even if we'd had full power we'd lost petrol in the attacks and didn't have enough to reach anywhere friendly. I thought the gunner was either dead or seriously wounded in the turret, so we had nobody to operate the wireless even if it was still working.

There was no choice, really. Ditching in the North Sea with no means of letting anyone know where they were, could mean days and nights in the dinghy, assuming that was still serviceable, with no good chance of being found. It was still usual for a squadron to mount searches over the sea if a crew was known to be lost out there somewhere, but no searches would have been made for Oates because there would have been no messages. To be found, by British, Danish or German, would have been a matter of pure luck. Oates turned back to attempt a forced landing.

Before he could find a suitable place to do that, the fighters found him again flying conveniently into view, and tried to force a landing of a different sort. Oates remembered 'flying up the street of a small town and under some telephone wires'.

Well, that's one way of putting it. The small town was Vester Torup, three miles from the coast, and Oates was having to fly like a mobbed sparrowhawk, twisting and turning in desperation, bullets coming at him continuously and ricocheting off the village houses. Being unable to strike back, with only one fully functioning engine and parts of his wings missing from the flak attack so long ago – all of fifteen minutes – he knew that if he carried on for only one more minute, they would be shot out of the air and would all probably be killed. So, while he still had some measure of control, he decided to crashland wherever he could, right now. With remarkable coolness, he switched on the fire extinguishers and headed down for he knew not what.

His aerobatics had taken him back towards the coast, towards the Torup Strand, and he was less than a mile from ditching in the Lundfjord when he hit his landing ground, a rough field east of Vust, and the impact knocked him out:

'After the crash I recovered consciousness [still in his seat] to see the gunner [Sgt Tom Graham] walking about but he was too dazed to know what he was doing. Biden was trapped forward of the cockpit. We were very lucky not to catch fire. I was paralysed from the waist down but not in pain.'

Oates had severe spinal injuries, cracks in his skull and various other wounds. Biden was better off but not by much, while Graham just had a few scratches. With no possibility of escape in this flat, bare countryside, his presence well advertised to the Germans, it was decided that Graham should stay with the aircraft and destroy anything that might be useful information for the enemy, while the other two sought to benefit from the help that appeared to be arriving. Oates remembered: 'Two Danish farmers lifted Biden and me out of the aircraft and an ambulance took us to Fjerritslev hospital, where we were treated liked heroes.'

And then there were none.

Here is the official German first report of the incident, before all the data had been collected and analysed:

At 12.16 there was an attack by 11 Bristol Blenheims on Ålborg West airfield, during which five were shot down in flames; in addition a further three were brought down by fighter planes; the rest flew off to the west. These machines were also said to be shot down by fighters.

Damage: so far the following has been reported: one Danish worker killed, six wounded, slight damage to the runway.

So far two officers and two other ranks captured. The others are said to have fled.

Later, two more of the Danes died of their injuries. There were no German casualties. Eyewitness accounts were reported in the local newspaper *Ålborg Stiftstidende* (*Morning News*). The Germans of course censored the Danish press but were very happy to give free rein to journalists when they had such good news to write about.

A man who worked in the Norden cement factory heard the air-raid siren and ran for the shelter. On his way, he heard and saw some of the fight.

As I left the factory the first rounds fired from the AA guns could be heard. I saw about ten English bombers coming from the south, in two formations, at about 1,000 metres heading west. Before they could reach the airfield they were met with many shells, and I saw fighters in the air too. The fighters attacked and scattered the rear formation. One bomber had its tail shot off and dived vertically into the earth. Another bomber was set on fire over Egholm island and an airman jumped from it with parachute. Yet another bomber was hit and crashed. This all happened in a few moments and then it was gone, out of sight. For as long as I live, I shall never forget what I saw that morning.

Another citizen of Ålborg had a view from a different angle:

I watched one of the bombers being hit and it seemed like it broke in two. There was smoke and fire and it went down at a terrible speed. I could see the crew trying to bale out but one had his parachute cords tangled and hit the ground with the aircraft. Other airmen were more successful and glided down into the fjord, where they were rescued.

The *Morning News* reported:

On Egholm island the farm workers were busy with harvest when the flak guns started up, frightening the horses, which tried to break free from their reaping machines and carts. Many witnesses saw a bomber fall into the sea, only a hundred metres from the shore and in shallow water. In the middle of the wreckage, three men could be seen, unable to move. The islanders waded out and found the airmen very badly hurt, one with broken limbs, all with severe facial injuries and bleeding profusely. They were taken by the emergency services in boats to a landing point at Ålborg and transferred to hospital.

This can only have been Blair, Magrath and Greenwood in R2772. Back in town, a reporter from the *Morning News* happened to be on his way to the police station as the air-raid sirens were wailing.

The English bombers came from the south and passed over the city in finger formation at a height of 1,000 metres. AA shells exploded round them like small clouds of wool against the blue sky. There was so much smoke that, for a moment, there seemed to be fifty aircraft up there. One of the bombers was hit and a yellow flame came from it as it fell out of the formation in a dive. It levelled out and carried on towards the target but only for a few seconds, when it rolled and dived again in a ball of yellow flames. Faster and faster it hurtled down until it crashed in a great red and yellow fire that could be seen for miles, while behind it a lone parachutist slowly descended to the ground.

As A Flight tried to make its escape, heading north-west towards the coast from the aerodrome, hotly pursued by fighters, they flew over the small towns of Kås and Pandrup, where many folk turned out to watch in fascinated horror. An eyewitness from Pandrup:

I heard a furious and thunderous roar and saw a

bomber going flat out, hunted by three fighters that jockeyed for position so they could hit the bomber in its weakest spots. It was like the most dangerous stunt flying display. At one moment the fighters were above the bomber, then again beneath it, or all around it. They were shooting continuously. I could hear the guns, and the bomber fired too, in short bursts, as it dived, climbed, and turned at impossible angles, and then it all stopped. The bomber stalled and fell, straight down to the ground, and exploded on impact, a massive explosion as if its bombs had gone off as well. Only the tailfin was recognisable from the wreckage. The crew also must have been entirely blown to pieces.

As we watched this terrible sight, another bomber appeared out of a cloud, chased by fighters in furious combat with fire coming from everywhere. How could the heavy English machine defeat its light and agile enemies? It was hopeless, and soon there was smoke coming from the bomber but this one did not go into a vertical dive like the other. It began to glide down, with a trail of smoke behind. A white spot appeared and was falling, whirling, and everyone was praying for the airman. At last his parachute unfurled and he landed in a meadow. Immediately there was a second parachute, emerging from the cloud where the aircraft had been, which was now smashing into the ground, turning somersaults and bursting into flames. While the second airman landed safely, we found the third one, lying beside a ditch. He had on his flying helmet with intercom. There was nothing we could do. He had been killed instantly in the crash, or perhaps was already dead from the fighting.

In a cornfield near Kås, one man had a very difficult job trying to calm his horses when a Blenheim crashed to the ground in the next field. This had been watched by another worker who had jumped into a ditch as the bullets flew over his head.

> The fighters came in from behind the bomber, firing like mad. Suddenly, the British machine fell like a burning rocket and hit the ground with a violent bang. I ran to get my bicycle, thinking that it was all over, when another combat arrived and I jumped back in the ditch. This other bomber was also set on fire but it fell slowly, and the crew were able to bale out. I saw four more bombers being chased westwards, and two of them went down in my sight, somewhere around Koldmose.

The last episode in this fantastic drama was witnessed by a citizen of Vester Torup, who saw a bomber coming back overland from the sea.

> It seemed as if the British aircraft had very bad damage. It flew very low, seemingly among the roofs of the houses. The fighters attacked and there was mayhem between the chimneys. Everything in the

village shook. Machine gun bullets whistled through the streets and people took shelter, as the combatants flew this way and that. Eventually, the bomber had to give up, landing in a field east of Vust. The pilot was badly injured, the observer less so and the gunner not at all, and he stayed with the machine until the Germans turned up. There were huge holes in the wings which apparently were the result of fire from the guns at the aerodrome.

Perhaps, without those holes, and with enough petrol, and with two serviceable engines, that was one Blenheim that might have got away. We cannot be sure of every aircraft these eyewitnesses were reporting, and it's hardly surprising that in the frenetic midst of the battle the fate of one crew and machine has been mixed with another. Even so, we can say that it was Sergeant John Oates in T1889 who was flying between the chimneys, the only one of A Flight to be seriously damaged by flak but, like all of that flight, ultimately a victim of the fighters.

The German press initially reported the Ålborg incident as two separate raids, by twelve and eleven bombers respectively, of which sixteen were shot down. The occupier's influence on the Ålborg *Morning News* editorial was also clear:

'Some Danish people were wounded during the attack but only a few were wounded seriously and two of them died later. Bombs that were dropped in a field killed some horses and cattle.'

Curiously, this is not the only news source to state that

there were twelve British bombers, of which one 'returned to England', even though Sgt Baron turned back before reaching the coast.

When Baron got home, the fact of his return would not have been questioned. Orders covered this type of decision, to return for perceived technical reasons. The preservation of crew and aircraft was an important matter to be balanced against the likelihood of failure due to a handicap in machinery or sickness in a crew member. Confirmation of Baron's account would be had from his CO, Wing Commander Lart, when everybody else returned.

But there was no confirmation, not even from his crew. They would have heard the conversation with Lart, but they could not have seen the petrol gauges at the time. When fuller news of the disaster reached the station, Sgt Baron's story was put in doubt and he was placed under open arrest, awaiting court martial for cowardice. The shame and stress of such treatment can hardly be understood by outsiders. It was, if such a thing can be, a fate worse than death. His crew at Ålborg on 13 August, Sgts Mason and Marriott, were flying again on ops on the 15th. Eventually, Norman Baron would be cleared of all charges – see Postscript.

The disastrous news was incomplete because some of the bodies could not be identified. It was not until 1946 that Edward Lart's family were able to obtain formal confirmation of his death and the circumstances of it. The Danish report at the time stated: 'Crew of three men dead, mutilated and charred. One identified as P/O Gillingham.'

R.A.F. Form 541.   123

OPERATIONS RECORD BOOK.

Appendix

DETAIL OF WORK CARRIED OUT.

By No. 82 Squadron, Watton.

No. of pages used for day

From 13 / 8 / 40 0840 to 13 / 8 / 40 1314

Aircraft Type and No.	Crew	Duty	Time Up	Time Down	Details of Sortie or Flight	References
Blenheim IV	S/Ldr. Wardell.	High Altitude formation raid on AALBORG			These 18 aircraft set out to bomb AALBORG aerodrome in formation, over 20,000 feet if possible.	
R.3690	F/S. Moore.					
	Sgt. Girvan.				Only one aircraft returned whose captain, Sgt.	
R.3821	P/O. Hale.				Baron, turned back owing to lack of petrol.	
	Sgt. Oliver.					
	Sgt. Boland.					
R.3915	Sgt. Baron.					
	Sgt. Mason.					
	Sgt. Marriott.					
R.3800	F/Lt. Syme.					
	Sgt. Wright.					
	Sgt. Turner.					
R.1935.	P/O. Parritt.					
	Sgt. Youngs.					
	Sgt. Newvuron.					
R.2772	Sgt. Blair.					
	Sgt. McGrath.					
	Sgt. Greenwood.					
T.1934	W/Gr. Lart.					
	P/O. Gillingham.					
	Sgt. Beeby.					

The Recorder of Operations was clearly a man of few words - but this is how they did it. Other reports would be rather more detailed, but the ORB was for facts only.

Although Dr Christiansen of Brovst hospital recovered a badly damaged pocket watch with the initials ASB on the back, the body of Gus Beeby was too scorched and mangled to be named.

Aircraft Type and No.	Crew	Duty.	Time Up.	Time Down.	Details of Sortie or Flight.	Reference.
R.3915	P/O. Wigley.					
	Sgt. Patchett.					
	Sgt. Morrison.					
L.1589	Sgt. Oates.					
	P/O. Biden.					
L.1827	Sgt. Graham.					
	S/L. Jones.					
	P/O. Granidge.					
R.3904	Sgt. Bristow.					
	P/O. Newland.					
	Sgt. Ankers.					
R.3902	Sgt. Turner.					
	F/L. Ellen.					
	Sgt. Dance.					
	Sgt. Davies.					

The same was true of Earl Hale and others. Twenty men died on the raid. At the time, it was not clear that the total was so high, as investigators could not separate mortal remains into twenty individual bodies. Without knowing how many men they were burying in a communal grave, the Germans

```
                                    Wing Commander E.F. PIPPET,

                                    123 STAGING POST
                                    ROYAL AIR FORCE
                                    TRANSPORT COMMAND
                                    KASTRUP LUFTHAVEN
  Reference: -                      COPENHAGEN
  EFP/DO.                                        B.A.F.O.,
                                    c/o B.A.O.R.
                                    6th March 1946.

    Dear Group Captain.

            With reference to your letter 46G/RHGN dated 10th January, 1946
    I am sorry that there has been such colossal delay in replying but I had
    to apply to the local M.R.E.U. and get them to carry out the necessary
    reconnaisance.

            The information they obtained is sketchy and leads one to the
    conclusion that the raid on which he lost his life was one of our more
    disorganised efforts.

            Approximately 150 people have been interrogated but due to the
    great time-lag between the incident and the inquiry nothing definite and
    clear out could be obtained.

            On the morning of 13th. August, 1940 a number of Blenheims
    crossed the AALBORG area causing an air raid alarm from 12.16 hours to
    12.40 hours.   Eleven of the Blenheims were shot down, five by flak, and
    six by a fighter.

            At a spot near AALBORG the wreckage of two burnt out Blenheims
    was found afterwards.   In one of these was found the burnt out remains
    of a gold watch bearing the name SGT. BEEBY.

            It is known that Sgt. BEEBY was the W-Op/A.G. of the crew of
    Blenheim 1934, of which W/Cdr. E.C. de V. LART was the pilot.   The
    Navigator was apparently a P/O. M.H. GILLINGHAM.

            Altogether there were eleven badly wrecked and in many cases
    burnt-out Blenheims in the area.   The remains of approximately fourteen
    British airmen were taken to the Chapel of the "Kommune Hospital" at
    AALBORG.

                    The/
```

'One of our more disorganised efforts', indeed. Confirmation of Edmund Lart's death was not obtained by his family until six years after the event.

held a full military funeral on 16 August with a 36-rifle salute.

What news of the boys in the British papers? *The Times* of 14 August carried a report under the headline 'Jutland to the Bay of Biscay – Counter-offensive by RAF – Daylight raids'. The text mentioned medium bombers carrying out daylight operations against enemy-occupied aerodromes and named

- 2 -

The bodies were so badly smashed up that it was impossible to say whether they represented fourteen or eighteen persons. There were nineteen airmen unaccounted for on this raid.

These remains were buried in a mass grave at VADUN, together with ten airmen from other crashes.

A memorial has been erected and paid for by the local people. This takes the form of a great stone wall with twenty-four memorial tablets in it, ten of which bear names, the others have been left blank until the names of the supposedly fourteen men could be established.

It has been suggested by the M.R.E.U. that one joint cross should now be erected on this grave.

It seems evident from this information that W/Cdr. LART lost his life when his Blenheim crashed and caught fire near AALBORG as a result of either enemy fighter or flak attack. It is not possible now to say whether the aircraft was on fire before it hit the ground or to say just how he was killed himself.

It is evident however, that he led a raid with great gallantry, through impossible opposition.

Yours

E.F. PIPPET W/CDR.

Group Captain R.H.G. NEVILLE, O.B.E., M.C.,
c/o Headquarters, No. 46 Group,
Royal Air Force,
Bushey Hall,
Nr. Watford, Herts.

six of those airfields, but did not include Ålborg in the list nor anywhere else in Jutland. 'Twelve aircraft have not returned,' it said, which was true enough. One Blenheim of 114 Squadron was lost without trace in a raid on Jersey, and we know what happened to the other eleven.

CHAPTER EIGHT

TO TELL THE TALE, YOU HAVE TO LIVE

The farm worker who took John Bristow and Nellie Ellen to his barn was Alfred Nielsen. The airmen were keen on getting away, and the first stage was accomplished on bicycles supplied by Nielsen. Bristow:

> He led us along country lanes for a few miles to a school building in a little place called Moseby, where we were picked up by the local GP, Doctor Bryder, who put us in the back of his car with a blanket over us. He drove us to the other end of the village, to the Jørgensens' house, where Mrs Jørgensen made us a lovely meal and gave us real coffee, which was a rarity in England even then.
>
> They put the wireless on to the BBC, and there were reports of a big battle over the Channel, with

many Hun machines shot down, so we hoped it was
all true and made up for us a bit.

This was Eagle Day, and in a way it more than made up for
82 Squadron. The weather, of course, had been the same for
the Luftwaffe and their massive fleet of bombers and fighter
escorts, intent on destroying RAF fighter bases, had been
recalled because of the heavy cloud over Britain and the
North Sea. The message reached the escorts and most of the
bombers but not all. Some heavy damage was done to several
RAF airfields, although they were not the intended fighter
bases, but the bombers with no fighter protection suffered
great losses to RAF Spitfires and Hurricanes.

Further attacks were launched and fighting went on for the
whole day, so the BBC news heard by John Bristow could
only have had early reports from the morning's episode of
the Battle of Britain. The final totals given by the Air Ministry
were 69 Luftwaffe aircraft down for 13 RAF fighters; later
consolidated figures indicated 47 against 13.

Danish hospitality was warm and welcoming but it could
not last. Everybody was well aware of the punishment likely
for those who sheltered enemies of Germany, and everybody
seemed to include all the children of the village who came
to look at the English heroes. John Bristow remembered the
awful threat: 'Mrs Jørgensen was quite rightly frightened that
the Germans were out looking for us and might turn up at
any time. If they found us having coffee and cakes, they'd take
the whole family away and very probably shoot them.'

As stated earlier, Germany would respect the freedom and

independence of the peoples of Denmark and Norway, and hoped very much that such respect would not be prejudiced by anything as silly as resistance, passive or active. Which is to say, we'll shoot you. Bristow: 'So, they decided to get in touch with the aerodrome and the Germans came for us. We hadn't really had a chance of anything else. Maybe if we'd melted away with Mr Nielsen we might have made it.'

Maybe, John, but the only hope would have been a boat to Sweden. Later in the war, when the Danish resistance was more organised, such a thing might have been possible, but not in 1940 and only a few months after the Occupation. Bristow continues the story:

They kept us at the aerodrome overnight, then put us on a Junkers 52 [a pre-war three-engined passenger and freight liner] for Hamburg. The other passenger was a German general. We were interrogated in Hamburg. The questions included date of birth and I told the officer, August 14th. 'But that's today,' he said. 'How wonderful,' and he sent his secretary out to get a bottle of schnapps, and we had a birthday drink, wishing each other good health. I suppose that, at the time, the Germans thought they were going to win the war and so could afford to be magnanimous.

Bill Magrath was not having anything like such a good time. He, Don Blair and Bill Greenwood, after their journey by straw-filled cart and rowing boat, were placed in a small field hospital in Ålborg. Newland, Syms and Wardell were there too. Magrath: 'They called it a clinic but I got no treatment at all for a whole week. I was in a bad way, and then they put me on a stretcher in the back of an army lorry and drove me to another hospital in Schleswig, which nearly finished me off.'

This was surely not typical of the way injured enemy airmen were treated by either side, and at Schleswig Bill found a more sympathetic regime, with a German army surgeon, Kapitan Doktor Marosy. Magrath:

> He did what he could, which involved sorting out my arm and my leg and lying in bed with them stretched out before me in plaster. It still hurt a lot, and I couldn't see out of my right eye. Anyway, there came a point when there was nothing more they could do with their limited resources and they sent me to a consultant orthopaedic surgeon at another hospital. He operated and did the job properly, which meant I could expect to be able to walk after a fashion and wave my arms about.

One night there was an air raid:

> I don't know if there were any shelters but I couldn't have gone anyhow, and a bomb exploded near us and blew the window in where I was, and threw my bed across the ward. Everybody else was either Polish or French, and they thought the bombs were great, and sang God Save the King while they were pushing my bed back and arranging my limbs in proper

order. Not long after that, I went back to Schleswig and discovered John Oates, who'd been the boss's wingman in A Flight.

Oates had been at Fjerritslev hospital, where the Danish staff had treated him like royalty, but he found Schleswig rather different:

> I'd been ten weeks with the Danes, then I was taken by ambulance to this muck-hole, still paralysed and so not able to help myself to do the basics. If there were any doctors there I didn't see any, or maybe they thought I was a hopeless case. The guards certainly thought so and used often to leave me on my own for days, so I couldn't go to the bogs or get a proper wash, not that I had a towel or soap anyway, or a comb. I was in a very dirty state, then two young Wehrmacht boys came in and asked why I was lying in my own filth, because the Germans did not treat airmen prisoners like this. They came back with a stretcher, took me up two flights of stairs and gave me a hot bath, and fed me with milk and fried potatoes.

Another move, to a hospital at Obermasfeld, did little to make life better for Oates, despite the British medical staff there. It had been set up centuries before as a hospital for the poor, but Oates simply found it a rather poor hospital as the medics decided it was too late to treat him. Oates:

One day, the Germans were going to take us walking wounded and blind out for a stroll in the countryside. This didn't suit one British officer who ordered me to march the men properly, to show the Germans how we did things. When I refused, he tried to court-martial me. I said that might be rather difficult in a German hospital but he was welcome to try it when we got home, then we could all have a good laugh.

At another camp near Kassel, an invigorated Oates made himself bookmaker at the fortnightly dog races. So successful was he that he ended up with all the *lagergeld*, all the prisoners' money, so he had to dish it out again to keep his business going.

Matters improved a little when Oates was taken to Stalag Luft 1, Barth, in the very north of Germany, and put in sick quarters:

The commandant came in one day, Major Burkhardt, and told us that Germany had invaded the Soviet Union [Operation Barbarossa, 22 June 1941]. I said something uncomplimentary concerning Napoleon and the 1812 Overture. Herr Major said nonsense, it would be over in six weeks, and bet me a bottle of cherry brandy against fifty English cigarettes. And, he said, if the Ivans weren't beaten, Germany would lose the war. I wrote the bet and the date on the wall. Six weeks to the day, he marched in, clicked heels, saluted, Heil Hitlered, put the brandy on my bedside locker, turned smartly and marched out.

Magrath was here too; both he and Oates were invalids and as such a burden on the Germans. It looked clear enough that they could never fly on active service again and so were prime candidates for repatriation. Indeed, they were told they were being sent to Switzerland, but the train they were on was clearly not going that way and they were disembarked at Schildberg (German name at the time for Ostrzeszów in south-west Poland). Oates:

'It was yet another staging post, and yet another hospital without doctors, nurses or treatment. There were hundreds of Allied wounded there, and a hundred fleas for each one. At last, the International Committee of the Red Cross formally passed Magrath and me for going home, and we were put on a train for Rouen.'

At Rouen was a POW transit camp built on the old racecourse. More than a year had passed since Ålborg and the two men were still in an awful state physically. Bill Magrath's mental state deteriorated too, when he heard that the verdict on his and Oates's repatriation had been reversed. 'I couldn't stand the thought of going back to a POW camp in Germany so I crewed up with a pilot from 83 Squadron and we decided to escape, which looked as if it might be a lot easier in France than it would be from Stalag Luft whatever. We liberated a set of wire cutters from a French electrician and went for it.'

Bill Magrath's companion was Sergeant Oliver Barton

James, who had been pilot of a Hampden bomber on a dawn mission to lay mines in the Bay of Biscay. Shot down at Morlaix, which is about 50 miles east of Brest in Finistère, James had serious injuries while two crew were killed and one got away. During James's hospital treatment, the German doctors decided he had to have his left arm amputated, so that made him an unlikely companion for one who had only recently learned to walk again. It was night-time, 21 November 1941. The camp was divided into three areas – officer prisoners, other ranks prisoners, and German staff. Magrath:

There were two other RAF fellows with us, both able-bodied, and we soon cut through the barbed wire that separated us non-officer prisoners from the German guards' quarters. We half expected to bump into some but they were all in their huts. We could hear them talking and laughing while we walked straight out of the gate. Once we were clear, we split into our pairs, and I limped off with my one-armed friend and headed south.

They had a vague idea of getting to Paris, where they thought they might find help from the resistance, but soon realised that help was required more immediately.

After four nights of walking, our food had run out and we were exhausted, well, I was anyway. James could have gone on on his own but we were probably better together, especially as I had my schoolboy French and he couldn't speak a word of it. We went into a village church and sat there, waiting for a miracle.

The miracle arrived in the guise of the local priest who, paying close attention to Magrath's story, understood enough of it to guess what was wanted. There were no Germans in the village so they could walk openly to the priest's house, the two airmen still in their uniforms, tatty and worn but dangerous nevertheless. 'The priest's housekeeper cooked us a meal, which was the best food we'd had for months, and boiled water for us to have baths. There was a comfortable bed too, and we slept the sleep of the just that night.'

The decision was taken that, despite the risk of being shot as spies if arrested, civilian clothes would replace RAF issue. The good Father went around to a few reliable people, collecting outfits for his refugees, and the housekeeper burned their cast-offs. Now there was a problem. Many more days of walking were out of the question, so a train to Paris had to be their option, but the station at the nearest town was continuously watched by German soldiers. The priest came up with an ingenious solution. Magrath:

It was brilliant, really. We hid a little way from the station while the priest, who had changed out of his clergyman gear into civvies, went in and replaced the clerk in the ticket office. We then trotted up, French workmen by all appearances, and without having to say anything were handed two third-class singles to

Paris. We passed over the money he'd already given us, and he handed back more in change than we'd had before. The Hun soldiers never noticed a thing. We couldn't say our goodbyes and thank-yous of course, but I'm sure the priest knew what we were feeling.

Arriving in the French capital with no knowledge of important matters such as the hours of curfew, no idea where to go, no identity papers and no understanding of the city's geography, Magrath and James wandered around hoping for some luck. The luck they had turned out to be mixed, starting well:

> The place was crawling with Germans, which was unnerving to say the least, and we couldn't work out what to do at all, until it began to get dark and we knew we had to sort something out quickly. Being on the streets at night would be asking for trouble. We saw a woman walking on her own in a quiet little backstreet and decided to chance it. I offered her money if she would put us up for the night, and she asked a lot of questions in rapid Parisian French, which I struggled with, but she must have realised that two crippled idiots like us could not be anything other than what we said we were. She took us home, gave us a meal and we kipped there.

Early in the morning, they set off for the usual first port of call for evaders, the local church. Their hostess had told them where the priest lived but they were too early for him. He was still in bed. So they tried the next church and the next priest, but he was the nervy type and quite petrified just by standing near two enemies of the Germans. Luckily he was equally frightened of the Germans and told the airmen only to *allez-vous en* as *vite* as they possibly could.

'There was a Metro station handy so I went to the kiosk and bought a Paris guidebook. James thought maybe we should try another religion and so, being C of E according to our RAF ID, we searched the map for the Anglican church we knew must be there somewhere.'

There were several. The nearest one was (and still is) St George's, rue Auguste Vacquerie, near l'Étoile, but it was closed. A notice on the door in English and French told them that services were suspended for the duration and that the building was under the jurisdiction of the American Embassy. This was only a few days before Pearl Harbor but the USA wasn't in the war yet and so represented nothing more than friendly neutrality. They found the embassy on their map and resumed on foot, not feeling confident enough to take the Metro. Magrath: 'We did wonder about the embassy. What arrangements might they have with the occupying power? Would they be obliged to hand us over? So when we saw a building with a Red Cross sign outside, we went in there instead.'

This was another gamble. Would there be anyone in authority in that Red Cross office who would be willing to risk compromising all their good activity just to help two British airmen get back home? In any case, neither of them looked as if they would be able to contribute much to the war effort if they did manage the journey.

The woman who met them at the door didn't take long to understand who they were and what they wanted. Quickly she ushered them in and along to a room that was a veritable hive of activity, with volunteers packing all sorts of goodies in parcels to be sent to victims of the war. Hopes rose when the woman gave each of the men 50 francs, with a bonus of two oranges, but fell rather sharply when a senior-seeming man turned up to ask them to follow him. Magrath: 'He took us up several flights of stairs, left us in a tiny attic room at the top of the house, and locked us in. As that key turned, we thought we'd had it. We sat on the floor and waited for the sound of jackboots.'

The more time went by, the better they began to feel. If they had been betrayed, surely the Germans would have been there in short order. So, when they did hear footsteps, and there was only one set, they looked up with moderate enthusiasm as the key turned and the door opened. What they saw was not quite what they'd expected. Magrath:

> It was a monk, of all people, in the full outfit. The French Friar Tuck, except more serious. Once he found out I claimed to be Irish, he thought he had a way of checking our story. Where was my school, how many of the masters were priests? Well, none of them, because it was Portora, in Enniskillen, one of King James's Royal Schools and firmly Protestant, but I told him we'd had a school trip to St Patrick's grave and that Oscar Wilde was an old boy, and that seemed to satisfy him. Then our original Red Cross

chap took us to his house, took us in as non-paying guests, and things began to happen.

The monk visited them several times, once with a camera and later with very authentic looking ID papers, well worn, showing them to be workers from Marseille returning home, which had the side effect of explaining to any curious Parisian Bill Magrath's unorthodox French accent. He was a country bumpkin from down south. They had train tickets to Nevers, on the border with Vichy France, unoccupied by Germans but officially a kind of German dependency, where they had to wait for the next stage of their journey to be organised.

Meanwhile, John Bristow had resumed his career as radio engineer. In his early days as prisoner at Barth, Stalag Luft 1, security had been fairly lax and working parties had been allowed outside the camp on parole. Barth was a sizeable town with many facilities including a shop that sold radios and spare parts, and Bristow asked someone on parole if he would have a look at the shop and see what might be acquired, such as valves. Just then a rumour went around that the working parties were to be stopped, so Bristow's man, not really knowing what he was doing, bought two valves.

These two components happened to be fine for the job Bristow had in mind, but there was nothing else. The working parties were soon forbidden so there was no source of supply. Bristow had no transformer to cut the voltage from the mains to suit the four-volt valves, no condensers, no resisters, and nothing with which to make an earphone. The list of camp bits and pieces employed by Bristow and his mates to make all these things is quite extraordinary: wire from the barracks lighting circuitry, tin cans, the heater from a discarded electric kettle, silver paper from cigarette packets, an aluminium billy can, greaseproof paper, a toothbrush handle, pencil lead, a Bakelite shaving box. Perhaps most remarkable of all, silver paper interleaved with pages from a bible and the resulting sandwich boiled in candle wax, made a condenser. According to Bristow, bibles were the only books to hand that had sufficiently high quality paper.

Bristow's colleague in all this was Sergeant David Young, WOp/AG with 43 Squadron flying Hampden bombers, who had been attacking aerodromes in northern France on the night of 6/7 December 1940 when he was shot down by flak, crash landed and all crew taken prisoner. Young had been a radio engineer at the BBC before the war and, according to Bristow, 'should never have been allowed to fly because he was far too clever'.

Interesting viewpoint; air chief marshals all take note. Young's theoretical knowledge, for example in doing the calculations that allowed them to transform German mains electricity into four volts DC, combined with Bristow's practical abilities, produced a wireless set, with one essential component missing. It worked, tuned to the 40-metre band on short wave, but they couldn't listen in because they had no earphone.

No matter how ingenious they were, the radio inventors could not make an earphone with bibles and pencil lead. The answer was to steal one. Although Bristow always felt guilty about it, the radio was paramount and so, when a certain Austrian security officer he had befriended invited him to his quarters for morning coffee, the chance was too good to miss. The officer was called from the room; Bristow swiftly disassembled the telephone earpiece, removed the essential parts and screwed the cover back on.

Desperate times call for desperate measures, and Bristow was sure there would be ructions, but no. Nothing was ever said. So, they heat-treated a piece of tin to soften it for a diaphragm, put the pieces together in a toothpowder tin, and there it was. Earphone Mark I, brackets, Barth.

There was an international system of coded correspondence. Certain prisoners' letters home would be taken to the Air Ministry and their seemingly innocent contents would be trawled for anything useful. Using this method, one of the prisoners announced the existence of the little wireless that would receive on 40 metres, and the Ministry set up a regular message service.

Bill Magrath and Oliver James had been at Nevers for three weeks, staying with various different people, including the local chief of police, while paperwork and tickets were arranged for Marseille and contact was made with the Pat O'Leary Line, an escape organisation that had its beginnings in June 1940.

Not all the soldiers of the British Expeditionary Force had sailed for home at Dunkirk. There were those who had been forced the other way, inland, as they fought rearguard actions in northern France and, when France fell, had no option but to flee southwards. The magnet was the sea port of Marseille but, without money or friends, or money to buy friends, they were stuck.

A Scottish minister had left his church in Paris and taken over the Seamen's Mission in Marseille, with permission from the Vichy officials who assumed that it would continue in its traditional role of providing spiritual and homely comforts to merchant sailors and fishermen. The minister, Donald Caskie, a crofter's son from Islay, added British military refugees to his responsibilities and the Mission soon became a busy safe house and a vital link in the newly created escape routes from France, over the Pyrenees and on through Spain to Gibralter. At first, almost all of the escapers were soldiers caught out by the rapid German advance. Later, they were almost all Allied airmen shot down.

One of the early helpers was Louis Nouveau. When the Mission was closed by the authorities for suspicious activities, Nouveau's apartment became a substitute safe house. Here for a while lived a quite remarkable man, a Belgian doctor, Albert-Marie Guerisse, who had gone to England with the BEF from Dunkirk, joined the Special Operations Executive, transformed himself into a French Canadian sailor called Pat O'Leary, first mate on a 'Q' ship on the Mediterranean coast, and became active in landing spies and saboteurs while taking evading airmen in exchange. He was arrested, escaped, came to Marseille, joined the organisation and, in October 1941, took over command when the previous leader was betrayed.

This was the set-up that gradually acquired his name as the Pat O'Leary Line, or just the Pat Line, and despite many betrayals and close shaves, continued in its work right into 1943. Infiltration by a double-dealing British criminal in December 1941, a petty crook called Harold Cole, almost finished it and many of its management, messengers and safe-house keepers were taken by the Gestapo. It was into this period of turmoil that Magrath and James arrived, to stay at Louis Nouveau's apartment.

The Germans knew full well that there were escape routes and escape organisations and, even without Gestapo interrogations of arrested members, they knew the jumping-off points for the way evaders had to go, over the Spanish Pyrenees. Perpignan, hardly 20 miles from the Spanish border, in that respect was a town that nowadays would be called a hub, and it was a hub for spies and collaborators as well as people-smugglers and those who made arrangements with them.

Magrath and James took a train to Perpignan on Christmas Eve, 1941, with a guide who was perhaps wishing that his two charges were not quite so memorable, one with a severe limp and one without an arm. He left them at a small, family-run boarding house that rejoiced in the name of Auberge d'Angleterre. Their hosts tried to give their guests an enjoyable Christmas but there was tension in the air. The recent arrests had made everyone jumpy, and the economics of escape had been somewhat altered by the announcement of a bounty of 8,000 francs for every evader turned in.

This meant that a smuggling mountain guide could get 16,000 francs for Bill and Oliver without having to go to all the trouble of guiding them through the Pyrenees in the depths of winter.

Such a sum would buy the guide 800 Reichsmarks, the main currency in many ways, which would have bought 4,000 pounds sterling in occupied Jersey. Quite what that would have meant in terms of bread, cheese and wine in Perpignan in 1941 it is very difficult to say, but it was a substantial amount of cash anyway.

The price asked by the guide/smuggler when he agreed to the job was 24,000 francs – three men's bounties, as it were. This was not unreasonable considering he was operating on a no-result, no-fee deal, because the whole of his payment awaited him at the British consulate in Barcelona. There remained the possibility of the three of them being arrested between Perpignan and the border, which would mean the guide being shot and the airmen getting the Gestapo treatment, and even when they got to Spain there were risks. The country was allegedly neutral but at this time, after the German invasion of the USSR, General Franco's anti-communist views ensured a pro-Germany bias among the authorities. If they were caught, Magrath and James could expect internment in a Spanish jail.

If they had read the tourist information they would have known that the eastern Pyrenees, where they were going, are particularly wild and naked, a chief feature being the rarity and elevation of the mountain passes. In winter, they were struggling through snow and high winds most of the way up and down. It took them two days to walk over, their guide obviously knowing what he was doing and dressed accordingly, while the airmen had nothing but their workmen clothes.

They fetched up in a small Gerona village, Vilajuïga, on 29 December, made it to Gerona itself, and were much relieved to be in the warmth and comfort of a railway carriage for the 50 miles or so remaining to Barcelona, where the guide had his reward, and from there to the British Embassy in Madrid.

John Oates the while was being moved from one unsuitable place to another. In transit with only one German guard, he had an overnight wait at Rostock railway station. The guard told Oates he came from Rostock, so Oates suggested he go and see his family. Guard and prisoner could reunite in the morning for the next train they had to catch, and prisoner could adjourn to the bar. Going outside for a breather in his RAF uniform, Oates was questioned by an Afrikakorps *feldwebel* (sergeant) who asked if he was Italian.

I said yes, I was, and was he Afrikakorps. He said yes, so I asked him how they were doing in Africa. 'Terrible,' he said, then wanted to know why I was laughing. I'm laughing, I said, because I am an Englander pilot, shot down. So what are you doing here, he naturally enquired, so I said I'd given my guard the night off, which made him laugh. We went back to the bar and had a few beers. War can be ridiculous sometimes.

82 SQUADRON AIRCRAFT AND CREWS AT GEMBLOUX AND ÅLBORG

List given in order of pilot, observer, WOp/AG. κ = killed in action.

17 May 1940

L8858 UX/W returned to base
Sgt T Morrison
Sgt Carbutt
AC1 Maison Charles Cleary (later F/Lt, DFM)

L8830 UX/T
F/O R J McConnell POW
Sgt S J Fulbrook evaded
LAC H Humphreys POW

P4838 UX/R. Crew commemorated at Runnymede

ᴋ F/O Alexander Moresby Gofton aged 29, son of Harry and Flora Gofton of Lae, New Guinea

ᴋ Sgt Frederick Stanley Miller, 27, husband of Emily May of Ewell, Surrey, son of Edward and Jane Miller

ᴋ Cpl Thomas Henry Cummins, 20, son of Thomas and Clara Cummins of Liverpool

P4851 UX/B. Two crew commemorated at Runnymede

F/O D A Fordham evaded

ᴋ Sgt Frank Fearnley, 24, son of Frank and Alice Fearnley of Baildon

ᴋ Cpl Allen Glyndwr Richards DFM, 20, son of Edward and Mary Richards of Caerau, Bridgend

P4852 UX/O

Sq/Ldr Miles Villiers Delap DFC evaded

Sgt R F Wyness DFM evaded

ᴋ P/O Frances Stanley Jackson, 22, husband of Kathleen Robina of Huntingdon, son of William and Elsie Jackson. Pancy-Courtecon cemetery

P4853 UX/D. Crew commemorated at Runnymede

ᴋ Sgt Reginald Edward Newbatt, 22, son of Henry and Drucilla Newbatt of Betchworth

ᴋ Sgt Joseph Kenneth Crawley, 24, son of Joseph and Elizabeth Crawley of St Helens

ᴋ Sgt Albert Vernon Knowles, 25, son of Albert and Elizabeth Knowles of Liverpool

P4854 UX/F. Two crew commemorated at Runnymede
   P/O Kenneth S Toft POW
   κ Sgt Arthur George Bernard Crouch, husband of Lilian
Marguerite of Leicester, son of Arthur and Kathleen Crouch
   κ LAC Raymonde Morris, son of Archibald and Ethel
Morris of Romford

P4898 UX/F. Crew commemorated at Runnymede
   κ P/O Severin Christensen, 21, son of Otto and
Catherine Christensen of Glasgow
   κ Sgt Alfred Norman Phillips
   κ LAC Peter Raymond Victor Ettershank

P4903 UX/U
   Sgt L H Wrightson evaded
   Sgt Stanley J Beaumont evaded
   AC1 K A Thomas evaded

P4904 UX/B
   Sgt T J Watkins evaded
   κ Sgt David John Lees, 25, son of Harry and Sarah Lees of
Erith. Lappion churchyard
   κ LAC Kenneth Gordon Reed, 19, son of Albert and
Elizabeth Reed of Penygraig. Merval churchyard

L9210 UX/O. Crew buried at Festieux Communal cemetery
   κ P/O James Joseph Grierson
   κ Sgt Joseph Wiliam Paul, 21, son of Thomas and Florence
Paul of Waltham
   κ AC2 John Hedley Patterson, 20, son of Joseph and Mary
Patterson of Hackney

L9213 UX/M. Crew buried at Presles-et-Thierney churchyard

ĸ F/Lt George William Campbell Watson, 26, husband of June of Cheltenham, son of Henry and Susan Watson

ĸ Sgt Francis Charles Wootten, 26, son of William and Annie Wootten of Cardiff

ĸ LAC Alfred George Sims, 25, husband of May, son of Percy and Ella Sims of Farnborough

13 August 1940. Those killed in action were buried at Vadum cemetery, about four miles north of Ålborg.

T1934 UX/R

ĸ W/C Edward Collis de Virac Lart DSO, 29, son of Charles and Amy Lart of Charmouth

ĸ P/O Maurice Hardy Gillingham, 22, son of James and Edith Gillingham of Hendon

ĸ Sgt Augustus Spencer Beeby DFM, 21, son of Oswald and Emily Beeby of Ashbourne

T1889 UX/L

Sgt John E Oates POW

P/O R M M Biden POW

Sgt Thomas Graham POW

R3913 UX/M

ĸ P/O Clive Warrington Wigley, 24, son of Frank and Kate Wigley of St Arvans

ĸ Sgt Arthur Homer Patchett

ĸ Sgt Archibald Finlayson Morrison, 31, son of John and Elizabeth Morrison of Glasgow

T1827 UX/H

ᴋ Sq/Ldr Norman Clifford Jones, 27, son of Joseph and Florence Jones of Holcombe

ᴋ P/O Thomas Johnson Cranidge, 26, son of John and Catherine Cranidge of Crowle

Sgt John F H Bristow POW

R3802 UX/A

F/Lt Ronald A G Ellen POW

Sgt V John Dance POW

ᴋ Sgt Gordon Davies

R3904 UX/K

P/O Benjamin T J Newland POW

ᴋ Sgt George Cyril Ankers, 24, son of George and Ann Ankers of Wombwell

ᴋ Sgt Kenneth Victor Turner

R3829 UX/S

Sq/Ldr R N Wardell POW

ᴋ F/Sgt George Percy Moore, 30, husband of Mabel of Llandrindod Wells, son of Harry and Miriam Moore

ᴋ Sgt Thomas Eckford Girvan, 19, son of William and Catherine Girvan of Dagenham

R3821 UX/N

ᴋ P/O Earl Robert Hale, 25, son of Robert and Maud Hale of North Vancouver

ᴋ Sgt Ralston George Oliver, 23, husband of Joyce Oliver of Exeter, son of Horace Florence Oliver

ᴋ Sgt Alfred Edward Boland, 24, son of Henry and Hilda Boland of Hull

R3800 UX/Z

F/Lt T E Syms POW

Sgt K H Wright POW

ᴋ Sgt Edward Victor Turner, age 20, son of Henry and Margaret Turner

R2772 UX/T

Sgt Donald Blair POW

Sgt William J Q Magrath POW, escaped

Sgt William Greenwood POW

T1933 UX/C

ᴋ P/O Douglas Alfred John Parfitt

ᴋ Sgt Leslie Reginald Youngs, age 21, son of George and Bertha Youngs of Diss

ᴋ Sgt Kenneth Walter Neaverson, age 28, son of Harry and Annie Neaverson of Doncaster

POSTSCRIPT

Flight Sergeant **Leslie Howard Wrightson**, husband of Mary, veteran of 17 May, was killed with 82 Squadron, 21 May 1941, flying from Malta, and lost without trace. Commemorated at Runnymede.

Sergeant **Thomas 'Jock' Morrison**, 27, husband of Mary, of Denny, Falkirk, son of William and Agnes of Stirling, veteran of 17 May, was killed 12 February 1941 in a non-operational crash.

Once his death was confirmed, Wing Commander **Edward Collis de Virac Lart DSO** was the subject of an obituary in *The Times*, in the form of a personal tribute written by his old CO, Group Captain Neville:

By the death in action of Wing Commander E de V Lart, DSO, the Royal Air Force has lost a most gallant and able officer, a fearless and inspiring leader, and a charming comrade. Edward Lart was a man of rare personality. His slight, rather delicate appearance, and his quiet, unassuming manner were apt to give a deceptive first impression; but it never took new companions long to discover his real quality, his great zest for action and his complete indifference to any physical danger, his exceptional hardihood and powers of concentration, and his extreme modesty about everything that he achieved.

With these qualities he combined considerable scholarship, an original mind, and a lively and subtle sense of humour. When this war broke out he was serving in the Middle East, but he never rested until he got home to have, as he wrote, 'a crack at Hitler'. His subsequent outstanding deeds, which led to the award of a posthumous DSO, have added gloriously to the great traditions of the Royal Air Force. Edward Lart's spirit lives on in those he has inspired by his example; and thus, although we may not see him, he is still with us, and his fine work continues in the Royal Air Force.

The crew that was replaced just before Ålborg – Wellings, McFarlane and Eames – had mixed fortunes. Squadron Leader **Donald Maitland Wellings DFC** was killed on 9 October 1944, when his Mosquito of 613 Squadron was shot down over The Netherlands. Flight Sergeant **Peter Kershaw Eames DFM** came back to Watton from his instructor posting and joined 21 Squadron. Flying with the squadron CO, Wing

Commander Bartlett, on 26 April 1941 his Blenheim was shot down by fighters over the North Sea, no bodies recovered. **Don McFarlane DFM** survived the war.

Sergeant **Norman Baron**, the one pilot to survive the Ålborg op, was cleared of cowardice at his court martial and returned to duty. He was posted to another Blenheim unit, 139 Squadron, based at Horsham St Faith, Norwich and, after a brief detachment to Malta, on to Oulton, Norfolk. His award of the Distinguished Flying Medal was published in the *London Gazette* on 8 July 1941. The citation stated:

In May 1941, Sergeant (Norman) Baron and Sergeant (Robert Walter) Ullmer, as pilot and wireless operator/ air gunner respectively, took part in an attack against a 6,000 ton enemy merchant vessel. Three direct hits were obtained and it was subsequently learned that the ship had been abandoned. A few days later, following a report that drifters were taking off the cargo, they again bombed the ship obtaining hits which caused smoke to be emitted. In June 1941, Sergeants Baron and Ullmer participated in an attack on a large and strongly escorted convoy. The particular section attacked consisted of six merchant vessels and six destroyers. Bombs from one of the leading aircraft struck two of the ships, one of which was an ammunition ship which blew up with terrific force and the aircraft in which Sergeant Baron and Sergeant Ullmer were flying was severely damaged by the blast. Despite the wrecking of his turret, Sergeant

Ullmer secured excellent photographs of the damage caused to the convoy and Sergeant Baron succeeded in flying the damaged aircraft back to base. Both airmen have consistently displayed great keenness, courage and determination.

Presumably they had different observers on these flights or there would have been another DFM awarded.

Twelve days after their awards were published, Norman Baron, still only twenty years of age, and Robert Ullmer, twenty-two, with observer Sergeant Kenneth Hopkinson, also twenty-two, took off from Oulton on an afternoon op against shipping at Le Touquet. They were shot down by flak and all three were killed, 20 July 1941.

Sergeant **Herbert Doughty**, who missed flying with Newland to Ålborg through being on leave, and whose replacement Ken Turner was killed, finished his tour of duty with 82 Squadron and was posted as an instructor to 52 Operational Training Unit. On 12 April 1941, he was in the crew of Blenheim L6790 on a local flying exercise when the aircraft, below the height authorised for the exercise, hit high tension cables near Crockey Hill, between York and Selby. All the crew were killed.

The aircraft had been built by A V Roe at Chadderton, Oldham, which was where Herbert Doughty came from. His younger brother, Joseph, trained as a pilot and was killed in a 9 Squadron Wellington, lost without trace age twenty on 9 March 1942. Thus it was for families with boys who wanted to fly.

Magrath and **James** eventually reached England via Gibraltar, only the third and fourth British servicemen to make it home after escaping from German imprisonment. They did it under great physical handicap and both were awarded the Military Medal in recognition of their extraordinary feat.

Magrath returned to flying duties at a training unit but was grounded by medical staff. No longer aircrew, he had to take a pay cut, which aggrieved him greatly. His case was taken up by a sympathetic officer and he was commissioned into the Administrative and Special Duties Branch where he trained in flight control. He left the RAF after the war as Squadron Leader Magrath MM.

Oliver Barton James, Bill Magrath's escape companion, was fitted with a prosthetic arm and as Flying Officer James MM, DFM, married to Sylvia, was killed on 4 October 1943 with 245 Squadron, 2nd Tactical Air Force, flying a Hawker Typhoon fighter attacking the retreating German army.

John Bristow continued his wireless-building career in Stalag Luft 3 and other camps. He and his magic contrivances were discovered several times but he just went back on the job and gained such a reputation that the Germans called him Radio Bristoff and kept a special eye on him. One of his inventions, a radio inside an accordion, was placed in a German museum. Two more, his billy-can radio, built inside a German mess tin, and his gramophone radio, can be seen in the museum at RAF Hendon. He also made models out of anything he could find, and even a medical device, a pneumothorax apparatus copied from a diagram in a medical book, which was used to treat prisoners with lung infections.

At the end of the war, he went through the same suffering as so many POWs, being force-marched from pillar to post by the Germans before being liberated by the British army.

Bill Greenwood, taken prisoner in 1940, passed some of his five years in POW camps by writing more letters to his pre-Ålborg favourite, the Hollywood singing star Deanna Durbin.

Dear Deanna,

Here I am writing to you once again but from Germany this time. I was shot down 13th August in Denmark and I am lucky to be alive because I came down in flames, then crashed. The only injury I have is my right ankle which was broken in three places by a bullet, but will be OK in another fortnight's time. When you answer will you please send me another snapshot of yourself because I lost all I had when I crashed in the water.

In this hospital where I am at present, we are well fed & treated. I don't have to work unless we want that is because we are sergeants. I hope you are still doing alright in films, and you will always be the tops with your looks & your voice you can't be anything else. I am looking forward to the day when you and I will meet, which will be another 5 years at the least, unless you come to England before that. I don't know what the weather is like in America, but here it is getting colder every day & another two or three weeks should bring the snow along. Would you please write to me every fortnight or at least once a month. I will be doing the same to you.

Close, wishing you and your FATHER and MOTHER the best of luck, Health and Happiness always.

Your Very Sincerely

Bill

Sgt. W. Greenwood, 646876, R.A.F. Dulag Luft Germany 3 Oct 1940

Air Force Transit camp B

And she did write too, and the correspondence continued, sometimes through an amanuensis but obviously enough to keep Bill keen. They never met, though, and Deanna Durbin – at one point the highest paid actress in Hollywood with the world's biggest fan club – retired from acting and singing in 1949.

John Oates was repatriated in 1943 via Sweden. As he left German custody, he was handed the ten shilling note that had been confiscated in 1940. He spent 18 months in hospital in England before rejoining his dairy firm. His camp commandant at Kassel had been a particularly civil and civilised man called Ritter. After the war, Oates wrote to him to thank him for his sympathetic treatment. When they met, years later, Ritter said that the letter had cleared him of charges of being a Nazi.

In 1943, the USAAF took over the **RAF Watton** base and built a concrete runway over a mile long, a perimeter track and fifty dispersal 'parking places'. It became the main depot for repairing and servicing the B-24 Liberators of the 2nd Air Division. It was also the base for the 25th Bombardment Group (Reconnaissance), which flew many special photographic and weather-information missions in advance of bombing raids. Their aircraft included the B17 Flying Fortress and de Havilland Mosquito.

After the war, the RAF used the station in one way or another for more than forty years, then the army had it briefly. It is now a housing estate and farmland although, at the time of writing, most of the runway is still there, as is the case with so many of the old USAAF bases in East Anglia.

In September 1995, routine works at Ålborg Airport uncovered some bits and pieces of metal that must have come from an aircraft. The airport's management were lucky to have such an expert on call as Ole Rønnest who, sure from the position of the wreckage that he was looking at **Blenheim R3821 UX/N**, had the initial concern that there might be unexploded munitions.

With the help of the army bomb-disposal people, the site was excavated and various aircraft parts were found that confirmed the identity of R3821. A few personal belongings were also discovered, including an identity bracelet engraved 'A E Boland S31257 C of E'. The bearer's religion – Church of England – on his ID bracelet was an instruction on the type of appropriate burial. There were human remains too. The Germans had not done a thorough job. These remains were interred at the Vadum cemetery.

In early 1941, **82 Squadron** was assigned mainly to attack enemy shipping in the English Channel and North Sea. A detachment was sent to Malta in May 1941, with the rest of the squadron following in June. Flying against shipping and ports, such heavy losses were suffered that the whole unit was brought back home.

No. 82 Squadron was moved out of Bomber Command in 1942 and sent to India to fight the Japanese, equipped with the American A-35 Vengeance dive-bomber, at first deployed on anti-submarine patrols and, later on, targets in Burma. Still in the Far East but now with the de Havilland Mosquito, the squadron was disbanded in March 1946, to be reformed at RAF Benson with Lancasters and Spitfires, then moved to African survey duties.

No. 82 entered the jet age in 1953 with the Canberra, to be disbanded again in July 1956, and reformed in July 1959 as a Thor missile unit. This type of intermediate range missile was made obsolete by the ICBM and the squadron was disbanded for the final time in July 1963.

BIBLIOGRAPHY

Barker, Ralph, *That Eternal Summer: Unknown Stories From the Battle of Britain*, Collins, 1990

Becker, Cajus, trs. and ed. Ziegler, Frank, *The Luftwaffe War Diaries*, Macdonald, 1964

Bowyer, Michael J F, *2 Group RAF: A Complete History*, Faber & Faber, 1974

Chorley, W R, *Bomber Command Losses of the Second World War*, Vol. 1, *1939–1940*, Crécy, 1992

Franks, Norman, *Valiant Wings: Battle and Blenheim Squadrons Over France*, Kimber, 1988

Middlebrook, Martin and Everitt, Chris, *The Bomber Command War Diaries: An Operational Reference Book, 1939–1945*, Viking, 1985

Passmore, Richard, *Blenheim Boy*, Harmsworth, 1981

Rønnest, Ole, *The Doomed Squadron* (*Den dømte eskadrille*), 2007

Alan J Brown's website: ajbrown.me.uk